KU-885-337

brilliant CV

What employers want to see and how to say it

Jim Bright and Joanne Earl

A CV should provide a brief but concise summary of relevant experience and competencies in a well-designed format that captures the reader's interest.

An imprint of **Pearson Education**

London · New York · San Francisco · Toronto · Sydney · Tokyo · Singapore
Hong Kong · Cape Town · Madrid · Paris · Milan · Munich · Amsterdam

PEARSON EDUCATION LIMITED

Head Office:
Edinburgh Gate
Harlow CM20 2JE
Tel: +44 (0)1279 623623
Fax: +44 (0)1279 431059

London Office:
128 Long Acre
London WC2E 9AN
Tel: +44 (0)20 7447 2000
Fax: +44 (0)20 7240 5771
Website: www.business-minds.com

_____

First published in Australia in 2000
by Business + Publishing

First published in Great Britain in 2001
by Pearson Education

© James Bright and Joanne Earl 2001

The right of James Bright and Joanne Earl to be identified
as Authors of this Work has been asserted by them in accordance
with the Copyright, Designs and Patents Act 1988.

ISBN 0 273 65485 3

British Library Cataloguing in Publication Data
A CIP catalogue record for this book can be obtained from the British Library.

All rights reserved; no part of this publication may be reproduced, stored
in a retrieval system, or transmitted in any form or by any means, electronic,
mechanical, photocopying, recording, or otherwise without either the prior
written permission of the Publishers or a licence permitting restricted copying
in the United Kingdom issued by the Copyright Licensing Agency Ltd,
90 Tottenham Court Road, London W1P 0LP. This book may not be lent,
resold, hired out or otherwise disposed of by way of trade in any form
of binding or cover other than that in which it is published, without the
prior consent of the Publishers.

10 9 8 7 6 5

Design by Claire Brodmann Book Designs, Lichfield, Staffs
Typeset by Northern Phototypesetting Co Ltd, Bolton
Printed and bound in Great Britain by Biddles Ltd, Guildford & King's Lynn

The Publishers' policy is to use paper manufactured from sustainable forests.

brilliant CV

for
John R. Bright,
Jean Bright and

the memory of **Beryl Bright**
and

for **Graeme and Isobel**

Contents

Acknowledgments

There have been many organisational psychologists, human resource managers and recruitment consultants who have provided us with great assistance in writing this book. We would like to thank Fiona Davies, Prue Laurence, Sonia Hutton – and Erin Stephenson, whose Masters and Honours research on CVs has provided us with invaluable help. Robert Bright was the human resources expert who started this all off – characteristically over a curry – with the simple question: What do we really know for sure about CVs?

Jenny Reddin and KODAK Pty Ltd supported our early work. Our research was supported tremendously by Dr Rob Anderson, Rachel Kenny and Jennifer Blake. Special thanks to Ms Doreen Cheong, who has guided our thinking on electronic CVs and co-presented seminars on this topic with us. Kevin Chandler from Chandler and Macleod Pty Ltd assisted us with the research on photographs and web-based recruitment. Many human resource professionals in Sydney and Melbourne assisted us by participating in our studies and reading through all the different CVs. Thanks to all our colleagues who have encouraged us in this project by reviewing our journal articles and even awarding us prizes!

The School of Psychology at the University of New South Wales (UNSW) has supported these studies and many of the staff there have provided useful feedback to us on the processes. Thanks to our collaborator Dr Austin Adams for his generous help.

Thanks also to Tim Edwards and the Woodslane team for all their support and expertise in developing this book.

Thanks also to the publishing team at Pearson Education in London: Annette McFadyen, Amanda Thompson and Rachael Stock.

About the authors

 **Jim Bright** (BA, PhD, MAPS, C.Psychol.) was born in Leamington Spa. He read Psychology at the University of Nottingham and received his PhD in Psychology in 1994. In 1995, Jim emigrated to take up his current position as a senior lecturer in organisational psychology at the University of New South Wales.

Jim works both as a scientist and as a consultant to industry. He has published numerous papers in international scientific journals on CVs in selection, training, motivation and stress. He consults to a wide range of organisations in the areas of career development, selection, testing and training. Jim is Chairman of the APS Sydney College of Organisational Psychologists, and is a regular guest on the Sally Loane programme on 702 ABC Sydney.

Jim's company, Jim Bright and Associates, offers a CV writing service – see www.jimbright.com.

Jim is married with a son, two cats and two dogs. In his spare time he enjoys walking Welsh springer spaniels and sailing.

Joanne Earl (BEd, BA, M.Psychol [Applied], MAPS) is a Registered Psychologist, a Member of the Australian Psychological Society (APS), a Member of the APS College of Organisational Psychologists and a member of the Australian Association of Career Counsellors. She has more than ten years' experience working in various human resources, training and psychological consulting roles. Her most recent work has focused on the development of on-line products to improve the recruitment and selection process.

She is married with a daughter, Isobel. In her spare time she reads detective novels, bushwalks and surfs the Internet.

Introduction

Remember your first date, or the first time you went out with your partner? Did you make sure your clothes were right, your hair right, you were wearing the right perfume or aftershave? Well, at least that much effort should go into getting your CV right! CVs are 'first dates' in the selection process that could land you on a new career path. Like the first date, they are the first time an employer gets to form an opinion about you – and first impressions can make all the difference. Employers routinely get thousands of CVs from candidates seeking the same job. That can mean odds of 1000–1 or even worse. A bad CV can reduce those chances from a long shot of 1000–1 to zero. A well thought-out CV can boost the same candidate's chance of being interviewed to one in three. Think about it: just by changing your CV, you can go from a situation where no one would interview you to getting interviewed on every third occasion. In some cases we are able to boost a CV so that the candidate is always interviewed.

Getting a job today can involve several steps, starting with a CV, followed by psychological tests and interviews. The CV is the only step where you have control over the information that you present. In every other step, the employer decides what questions to ask, what information to collect. The CV is your vital opportunity to present yourself at your best. CVs are important.

There are many different books on the market providing advice on CV preparation. This is the first book that gives clear, down-to-earth advice that has been shown scientifically to work. This book is the culmination of years of dedicated scientific research into what makes a winning (and losing) CV. We have interviewed hundreds of recruiters across a wide spectrum of industry and asked them to judge real CVs. The advice we now pass on to you is based on sound principles that have emerged from this work, and not on gossip, hearsay or anecdotes.

The aim of this guide is to provide you with no-nonsense advice about how to get the most out of your CV. It will increase your chances of being shortlisted for that all-important job.

We show you how to put together a persuasive CV. We give examples of CVs that work and those that don't and we explain to you why one works and another doesn't. We introduce you to some key job-seeking skills that will improve the quality of your CV. Every person has different strengths and weaknesses. The authors of *Brilliant CV* are organisational psychologists who understand these differences. Using simple exercises, we will show you how to tailor a CV to your strengths.

In the following chapters, we provide advice on the layout, content and construction of your CV and its covering letter. We also address some of the tricky questions:

- Do I explain gaps in my career history?

- Do I need different CVs for different jobs?

- Should I describe all my duties at work?

- Can I email my CV?

- Can I get any clues from the job advertisement that will improve my CV?

- Do I include a photograph?

- Can I leave stuff out of my CV and, if so, what stuff?

We are confident that this guide will assist you in producing the best possible CV. The recruitment industry has assisted us in all of our work, and the advice we pass on here is a reflection of our close relationship with the people who are making decisions about CVs every day. The results of our work have been published in several industry and international scientific journals, and have been presented at international conferences in Australia and the US. Training courses based on our work have been conducted in blue-chip companies.

How to use this book

This book is divided into four Parts. Part 1 introduces the concept of a CV as a marketing document, and leads the reader through a series of exercises to help them put together a thorough CV. Part 2 builds on this by showing the reader how they can enhance their CV to make it even stronger. Part 3 provides answers to some of those tricky questions regarding what to include and what to leave out, as well as issues such as referees, dealing with prejudice, the recruiter's thought processes during selection and using the Internet.

Finally, Part 4 provides a series of valuable resources to assist you in the preparation of your CVs, some example CVs, and some useful sources for getting more information on jobs and CVs.

Throughout this book you will see 'Recruiter's tips' indicated by tick boxes, thus ☑. All of these tips come straight from the human resource experts we interviewed and surveyed in our research programme, so you know exactly what the experts want to see! Throughout the book, and in the last section especially, you will see graphs, figures and tables that report data that have come straight from our studies, so at all times you are getting advice and the facts to back it up!

part one

writing a **CV** from scratch

The first part of the book is designed to take you through some of the fundamental stages in putting together your CV. It will be particularly useful for readers who have never attempted to put together a CV before, or for readers who have not done so recently. Of course, even if you have a basic CV, it never hurts to revisit the basics to ensure you are building from a strong foundation.

1 How to sell yourself

In this chapter, you will learn how to:

- make your CV a sales and marketing document

- sell yourself as the 'best buy' to an employer through your CV.

Andy Warhol said everybody gets their 15 minutes of fame. The CV is your opportunity to be in the spotlight, but unfortunately most candidates are lucky to get five minutes. It depends on the job and the number of applicants, but recruiters will, on average, spend less than two minutes reading a CV. They'll never admit it publicly, but it is not unheard of for a recruiter to send a CV straight to the waste paper basket with nothing more than a quick glance.

Your job is to make the most of that tiny window of opportunity to sell yourself to the recruiter. Your CV must sell, sell, sell! It must sell you.

 Remember that you are marketing yourself, so while the integrity of the document is a must, the CV must present your best experience and detail your relevant skills and competencies.

Standing tall

Some people come over shy and retiring when we tell them to present themselves at their best. For many people, it is not natural to be forthcoming and assertive. Our language is stacked with words and phrases that reflect this concern – 'blowing your own trumpet', 'bighead', 'up yourself'!

The fact of the matter is, you have to sell yourself. Do not think that employers will run to your door, overcome and enchanted by your modesty and understatement.

Still not convinced? Just consider all the other applicants. Will they be equally timid? You have to make your CV better than theirs. You have to make yourself better than them.

Hands up how many of you are thinking: 'Oh no, I'm being asked to go way over the top, and that's not me!'?

Remember, there are even more ways of selling things than there are ways of skinning cats (and most of them are a lot less noisy).

Don't lay out your life, warts and all, and expect a recruiter to be able to pick through your story, see your inherent skills and marvel at your honesty.

Consider the following three approaches to your CV.

Not selling yourself – too negative

'I did not enjoy college so I deferred and travelled around for a couple of years. I got to see a lot of different countries but eventually returned home, and I am now seeking a job...'

Good selling – turning negatives into believable positives

'After enrolling at college I was provided with an opportunity to join a crew sailing around the world. I accepted this once-in-a-lifetime challenge, which offered me invaluable lessons in the importance of teamwork, shared responsibility and leadership. I am now seeking to apply these skills...'

Bad selling – way over the top, unbelievable and undesirable

'I found I was not sufficiently challenged by the intellectual rigour of college life and left to pursue more appropriate ventures. I masterminded a round-the-world yacht race, and although there were other crew on board, most would probably agree I was the leader. I can now do wonders for you...'

The purpose of checking these three approaches against your CV is to make the point that you should not confuse selling yourself with telling lies, wild exaggeration or deliberately misleading someone.

Selling yourself is about being positive and persuading others to share this view of you.

Suppose you are driving with a friend as a passenger who is getting impatient and wants to know when you'll arrive at your destination. You are halfway there. What do you say to soothe him? If the journey were two miles, then saying 'Only another one mile to go' would sound better than 'We're only halfway there'. If the journey were 2000 miles in total, which would sound better: 'Only another 1000 miles to go', or 'We're halfway there already'?

Neither statement is untrue, nor misleading, but one serves your purposes well and the other does not. It is the same with CV writing.

If you cannot say something in a positive way, consider not saying it at all.

But how positive?

So, selling is important. That said, remember that selling is like perfume – a little used judiciously is attractive and enhances the person, but drown yourself in perfume and it is a big turn-off! The same goes for selling yourself: you need to know when to stop.

The following chapters will go into detail about how best to sell yourself, but before we move on, test yourself on our Over-the-top quiz.

Over-the-top quiz

Rate each of the ideas using the scale below:

1   The work of a sad and deranged mind.

2   Not me, but I know someone who would.

3   Hmm, sounds interesting, tell me more.

4   Who gave you a copy of my CV?

Now add your points and check your score. How did you do?

Make your CV stand out by using brightly coloured paper and a really **wacky font**	1	2	3	4
Get your CV delivered by a bikini-clad woman	1	2	3	4
If you are a bank manager, set out your CV like a cheque book	1	2	3	4
If you are an architect, design your CV in 3-D, in the form of a house	1	2	3	4
If going for a job in advertising, attach a condom to your CV ('I'm a SAFE bet...')	1	2	3	4

4–5 points   You will lead a long, happy and successful life. You were not tempted by these way over-the-top ways of getting a recruiter's attention. These approaches nearly always fail, despite any rumours you may have heard.

6–10 points   You are not a bad person, but you have some strange friends or are easily led. Good to see you would not use these methods, but you could offer to re-write the CVs of those who might be tempted.

11 points   Get help urgently! The help you need can be found below in the section on wacky CVs. Read it carefully and follow the advice!

16–20 points   To quote from *The Life of Brian*: 'It is people like you wot cause unrest.' Read the following section carefully, and for the sake of your job application, trust us, the wacky way is not the successful way!

The wacky CV

We have seen and heard of plenty of different 'way-out' CVs and, without exception, we would never recommend them. Don't be tempted, not even for a minute. Some of you might be saying, 'Well, what's wrong with that idea?', or possibly, 'But you haven't read my CV!' Let's look at each in turn.

A CV delivered by a bikini-clad woman

If you were going for a job as doorman in the *Playboy* Club circa 1975, this might just be a good move. Come on!

Anyone using a semi-clad woman to advance their application will probably be written off as insensitive and coarse at best, and mysogynist and chauvinist at worst. Questions of appropriateness and targeting the particular requirements of the position are discussed later.

Bank manager's CV set out like a cheque book

When has being a raging individualist been a prerequisite for working in a bank? A recruiter might ask themself why a bank manager needed to use gimmicks: what are they hiding? (And how would I get it in the photocopier?)

Architect's 3-D CV in the form of a house

This is a bit more understandable, but again, the candidate is risking appearing a bit twee or lightweight. And, of course, there are practical problems for recruiters receiving these sorts of CVs. How do they file or copy them easily?

Advertising candidate CV with condom attached

…Please!

Using coloured paper or unusual fonts

In a study we conducted with recruiters, all of them hated the unusual CV we showed them – it was on coloured paper and printed with a strange font. When we presented the same CV on white paper in a standard font, all the recruiters were impressed.

You will hear stories of people getting interviews and jobs that they think they got by using gimmicky CVs. These are exceptional cases – do not be tempted.

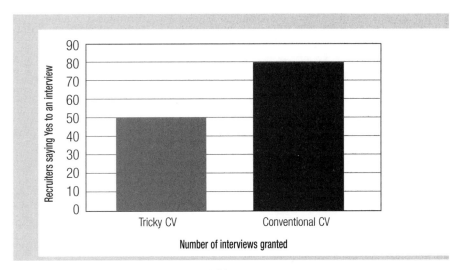

Figure 1   Recruiters' responses to unusual CVs

 Never be tempted to use an unusual layout, no matter what stories of success you hear.

Taste test

So, why do recruiters dislike 'wacky' CVs? The answers could fill another book, but there are some examples in life that reinforce this view. Firstly, there is good old taste. A painting by Picasso may be a great work of art to one person, and worse than a child's scribble to another. People's tastes differ. Many people tend to like things that are familiar. They also find them more memorable. It's sobering to recall that in a survey conducted in the UK recently, the most common response to the request to name an artist was 'Rolf Harris'!

Secondly, people's opinions differ. Just think about politics and sport. In most countries there are two or three parties that have widespread support and then lots of 'minority interest' parties. Think about the arguments that rage about the selection of sportsmen and women to national teams. How does all this relate to CVs? All we are saying here is that things that are unusual will attract attention – like a Picasso painting or an unusual decision by a selector – and in return will elicit a reaction, positive or negative. If you don't know how the reader will react, why run the risk of rejection unnecessarily?

2 The applicant–employer fit

In this chapter, you will learn how:

■ recruiters try to match CVs and jobs together

■ knowledge, skills, abilities and attitudes are used to fit people to jobs.

What is fit?

If you hang around with recruitment consultants for long enough (about two minutes is usually adequate) you will hear them talking about 'fit'. The way that they see recruitment and the way many firms think about it is in terms of getting a good 'fit' between the employer and the employee. Below is a diagram that illustrates this concept of fit.

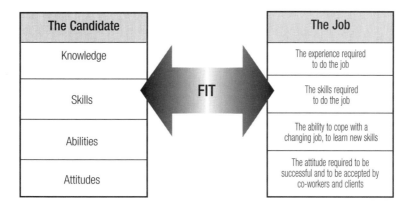

The Candidate		The Job
Knowledge		The experience required to do the job
Skills	FIT	The skills required to do the job
Abilities		The ability to cope with a changing job, to learn new skills
Attitudes		The attitude required to be successful and to be accepted by co-workers and clients

Figure 2   Factors in finding the right fit

As you can see from the diagram, fit is all about matching a candidate to a particular job. The best candidate for the job will be the one who who matches all the requirements of the job.

You can see from Figure 2 (page 11) that employers tend to think about 'fit' in terms of four different qualities:

1 *Knowledge* which refers to the experience and qualifications that you possess.

2 *Skill* which refers to the demonstrated skills you have (perhaps evidenced by your qualifications).

3 *Abilities* which show your potential to carry out a range of different tasks beyond your immediate skills or knowledge, and the degree to which you can take on new tasks successfully or be trained in new methods or equipment.

4 *Attitudes* which indicate your personality, and the degree to which you are enthusiastic, flexible and positive in approach.

It is clear when you look at Figure 2 that merely setting out your life history on a CV is highly unlikely to offer the best fit. This is why it is so important to tailor your CV to the particular position – to increase the fit between you and the job.

The following example illustrates this point. Below are three candidates who have applied for a sales job. From reading their CVs, the employer has listed each candidate's knowledge, skills and abilities on a grid, next to the job requirements. Which candidate fits the job best?

We think that Tim is the weakest candidate. He has the best academic qualifications, but these are unnecessary for the position offered. Although Tim could easily learn new skills and accommodate to changing demands in the job, the comment in Tim's CV, 'I am a strong-minded person who is not afraid to stand my ground in disputes', gave an unfortunate impression of someone who might be argumentative with the public.

Liz clearly has a lot of experience in retail, but in a very different area. There could be some concerns about her ability to deal with customers sensitively. There did not appear to be much development of new skills over the ten years, and little evidence that she would adapt to new payment processes easily.

Jane looks the strongest candidate to us. She has the necessary experience, and should be able to adapt to most new processes with training. She is not over- or underqualified for the job and seems the best prospect.

Applicants for a sales assistant job in a chemist

	Job requirements	Tim	Liz	Jane
Knowledge	Knows how a cash register works. Knows procedures for dealing with customers	*Degree in English, worked part-time in a burger bar for 18 months*	*Worked in father's hardware store for 10 years*	*Worked in a shoe store for 3 years*
Skills	Numeracy Good communication skills	*Easily able to handle cash and card transactions*	*Easily able to handle cash and card transactions*	*Easily able to handle cash and card transactions*
Abilities	To learn to process charge cards, electronic transactions	*No difficulties learning new skills*	*No evidence of learning new skills*	*Probably able to deal with new payment methods with some training*
Attitude	Polite, punctual, trustworthy, calm	*Strong-minded, self-confident, assertive*	*Honest, a bit aloof at times*	*Calm, honest, level headed*
Degree of fit		**POOR**	**AVERAGE**	**GOOD**

In this analysis you might think we have been terribly unfair to one or other of the candidates. Perhaps we have, but the point of this exercise was to illustrate the sorts of processes that recruiters go through in making decisions to shortlist applicants.

Improving the fit

When you set out job requirements as clearly as this, it is easy to see how you can start to mould your CV to match the job. Each of the candidates above could probably make themselves look the best candidate by altering their CVs. Below we offer some advice and we describe these changes in more detail in the following chapters.

Tim could turn that negative remark about standing his ground into a positive, by rephrasing it: 'I am a confident person, and I enjoy talking to customers, and helping the customer reach the right decision.' Tim could also put more emphasis on his retail experience and less on the education. Perhaps a 'career objective' statement outlining what Tim hopes to achieve would help persuade the recruiter that this was a serious career move for Tim.

Liz needs to make far more of her ten years of experience. There must be many achievements, and new skills that she has learned. These need to be emphasised on the CV. Jane looks pretty good already, but perhaps she could try to emphasise her abilities, or her potential to learn more, by providing examples of new skills she has learned over the past three years.

So now you've seen that CVs need to sell, and you know how recruiters use the best 'fit' as a guide to the best candidate. The next chapter shows you how to work out what recruiters are looking for – how to determine the job's requirements.

 Make sure your CV addresses the advertised position.

3 Where is the prime suspect?

In this chapter, you will learn to:

■ become a job detective

■ find out as much as you can about a job before applying

■ understand what an employer is looking for in a job advertisement.

Becoming a job detective

Imagine the scene: an office in the City, but there is someone missing from one desk. Witnesses say the missing person is dynamic, well qualified and pays exceptional attention to detail...

Every employer has a 'prime suspect' in mind when they advertise a position, and they tend to leave clues to that person's identity in their job descriptions. In this chapter we teach you to become a job detective, so that you can pick up all the clues and solve the mystery – what would the ideal candidate for this job look like?

To produce the best 'fitting' CV you need to know about yourself and you need to know about the job you are applying for. This chapter shows you how to work out exactly what the job is all about, and the following chapters then show you how to best mould your CV to the job to produce the best fit.

 CVs should always be written with the job in mind.

Job detectives question themselves

Before you do anything else, ask yourself why you are preparing a CV. The answer to this question is going to vary from one person to the next, but here are our top ten reasons for writing a CV:

1 You have seen a job advertised in the paper that appeals to you.

2 You want to market yourself to win a tender or a proposal, or be elected to a committee or organisation.

3 You have seen a job on the Internet job site that appeals to you.

4 Your friends/family told you of a job going at East West Ltd.

5 You want to work for East West Ltd and thought that sending a CV to them might get their attention.

6 You have seen a job advertised internally at work.

7 You are going for promotion.

8 You are about to be made redundant and want to update your CV to be ready for any good opportunities.

9 You are feeling fed up and writing down all your achievements will cheer you up and might motivate you to look for a better job.

10 Oh, so that's a CV! I've never done one. I suppose I ought to try to remember what I've been doing with my life!

All of these certainly are good reasons to write a CV, but the CV serves many different purposes. One way of seeing the differences is to ask yourself who is going to read the CV in each case?

CVs 1 to 5 are going to be read by potential employers who probably do not know you. A CV for 6 or 7 is likely to be read by your boss or other people who know you. CVs 8 to 10 are really for your own benefit and should not be considered as suitable for sending out to employers.

The right mix

Have a think about the list of reasons again. How else can you divide up these reasons?

A most important difference is that, in some cases, you will have a good idea of what the employer is looking for because you have a job advertisement in front of you and can tailor your CV accordingly. For others, you have no idea what the reader might want to see.

It is always worth updating your CV from time to time so you do not forget important details, but remember, the result of that process will not be a winning CV. It will be a useful list of tasks and achievements.

CVs are like baking cakes. You need all the right ingredients: flour, butter, eggs and so on. It is what you do with the ingredients that makes the difference between a great CV (or cake) and failure. Keeping your CV up to date is like keeping a stock of ingredients in the pantry – potentially very useful, but do not imagine that is the end of it!

If there is a most important piece of advice to give you, it is that you must think about what the employer is looking for and then reflect that in your CV. This advice was the most common tip from a large sample of recruitment managers.

Think about what the employer is looking for and then reflect that in your CV.

CV writing

You should tailor the information in your CV to the main points in the job advertisement. Okay, that sounds fine, but how do I do it?

Get as much information about the job and the company as you can. When you've got that, go and get some more! The main source of information about a job is normally from:

■ a job advertisement

■ a job description

■ a friend in the company

■ the media

■ gossip and rumour

■ someone already doing the job or something similar.

There is no substitute for experience. Talking to someone who does a job similar to the one you wish to apply for in the same company may well provide you with a good picture of what the job is really like. Bear in mind, of course, that this source of information is not always reliable. You may react differently to your friend, and therefore their experience of a company may be very different to yours.

However, a friend with reliable information can be a golden opportunity. Make sure you do not waste the chance to get some information. One way of ensuring that the information you get is useful is to use our job advertisement interrogation questions on page 20.

If you have friends who can provide valuable information – use them!

The main source of information about an employer's company is normally from:

- the media
- annual reports/company brochures
- industry/trade magazines or journals
- the Internet
- industry directories
- gossip and rumour.

There are many other sources of information about companies and if you're serious about knowing more about a potential employer (and you should be) it's worth a visit to your local library. Ask a reference librarian to help you with your search. It will help if you outline to the librarian that you are looking for information on a specific company to help with your job search.

Understanding an employer's WIIFT

When thinking about any employer, you should always be thinking about how they will see you and what benefits they may see in hiring you. This is known in the trade as the WIIFT, or What's In It For Them.

Understanding the company helps you to better understand the WIIFT, that is, the benefits of having you as an employee.

Do your homework prior to applying. Find out about the company, obtain an annual report if available, find out what future projects the company might be involved with, who their clients are and who their competitors are.

4 How to read a job ad

In this chapter, you will learn:

■ how to take the right information from a job advert

■ how to find out what the company does and what they want from you

■ what personal qualities you need to get the job.

The job detective examines the job advert

Job advertisements and descriptions should be treated as clues. Job advertisements are usually reliable sources of information and should be taken seriously. Employers can be found to have broken the law if they put misleading or incorrect information in advertisements.

Information from other sources can sometimes be invaluable, sometimes grossly inaccurate. The same principles apply whatever the source of the information.

Here is a typical job ad. Below it are our tips for reading the ad.

After reading the job advertisement, the seven questions below will assist in breaking down the job ad successfully. Remember, reading an ad properly is the first crucial step to preparing a successful CV.

Training Manager
Handle Sisters Pharmaceuticals

Would you like to join the world's 3rd biggest pharmaceutical company, currently expanding rapidly in the European market? We require a manager to join our training division, where you would be responsible for the delivery of training programmes to our sales staff.

A dynamic, results-focused team player, you will have excellent communications skills, and will be able to handle pressure and work to deadlines. With several years of solid experience in a multinational, you will be accredited in NLP and will have a basic understanding of training evaluation techniques. Reporting to our Regional Manager, you will be required to provide input into the marketing strategies for the European region by training our sales staff to improve market share.

Handle Sisters are Equal Opportunities employers.

Please forward your CV to: Linda Spark, Personnel Dept, Handle Sisters Pharmaceuticals, 58 Boundary Street, London EC1 2LP.

The seven job advertisement interrogation questions

1   What don't you understand about the job ad?

2   What type of industry/company is it? What's happening in the company or industry? Is it restructuring or expanding? Does it operate with low overheads and high profit margins?

3   What is the main purpose of the role being offered?

4   Why is this role important to the company? How will this role affect the company's bottom line?

5   What types of skills do they want? What other skills might be needed given the job's purpose?

6   What types of personal qualities do they want? What other personal qualities might be needed, given the job's purpose?

7   What types of knowledge/training do they want? What other knowledge or training might be needed, given the job's purpose?

Now that you have read the questions, we will take you through them one at a time.

1   What don't you understand about the job ad?

Here are some definitions to help you understand our example.

Equal Opportunities employer refers to a company that has policies of non-discrimination in the workforce on the basis of gender, ethnicity, sexual preference, age or other factors.

Neurolinguistic programming (NLP) is a controversial training technique that is intended to improve both verbal and non-verbal communication.

A general clue to the significance of these jargon terms can be gleaned from their positions in the ad. If the jargon words appear next to descriptions of qualifications required, it is a good bet that the words refer to skills you will need (such as NLP in this case). If the words appear towards the end of the ad where the contact details appear, or near a description of the company, then it is likely that these words refer to general conditions of employment or company policy (such as Equal Opportunity employer).

If you are still stuck, you could try contacting the Office of Fair Trading about the phrases that may have legal meanings, like Equal Opportunity employer. You could always contact the employer and ask, but if you think this may create a poor impression, get a friend to call instead.

If the terms are likely to refer to a technical aspect of the job, it may be worth visiting your library and searching for books on the subject, or contacting the relevant professional association or trade union (such as the Transport and General Workers Union, the Association of Chartered Accountants or the Publishers Association).

Other than standard reference works like dictionaries, thesauruses and encyclopedias, logging onto the Internet is a very powerful way to search for information. If you use the Internet, you can search for a particular keyword or phrase that you do not understand. Another good idea would be to try out some of the job web sites we recommend in Part 4. These contain explanations of work-related terms, and some carry profiles of different employers and company sections.

2   What type of industry or company is it and what's happening currently?

Some of this information can be gleaned from the job ad. In our example, the company seems to operate on a global scale as it refers to the 'European division' and asks for experience in multi-nationals. Secondly, it gives the impression it is expanding in that part of the world. However, this doesn't mean that it is expanding everywhere, and it doesn't say whether Europe includes the UK, where the correspondence address is. The job may involve overseas travel, or be based overseas. It is not possible to tell whether the company is restructuring or what its profitability is.

Information about companies can be gleaned from many different sources. Remember our earlier tip to visit your local library to review any existing information in such publications as *Financial Times Top 500 Companies*. Ask a librarian how best to conduct your search. It is easy to miss huge chunks of information.

Do you know anyone who works for the company? If so, talk to them. Could they get hold of any company brochures, newsletters or advertising material for you? In our example, you might ask if there is anything in the latest pharmaceutical trade journals.

If you are keen to work for a large company, start reading the business pages of the newspaper to see if there are any stories about the company. If it is a public company, you could always ask for a copy of the annual report. This may tell you whether the company is growing or not, how profitable it is, and whether any redundancies are planned.

Because this company sells pharmaceuticals, it might be worth going to a pharmacy to ask about the company, or asking a doctor. Then you might be able to find out if this company sells medicinal products. Also check out the supermarkets to see if this company sells domestic products such as soap powder. Take the job ad with you, so you can match the logo and address with the products on the shelf.

3   What is the main purpose of the role?

In this case, it is fairly clear that the main duty will be to conduct training of sales staff. Duties are likely to be fairly well known by job applicants, as the role needs somebody with experience and qualifications. However, training itself is a broad role that may involve many responsibilities. It may be that the company specialises in an industry that has very specific training needs. For example, a petroleum company may have to adhere to occupational health and safety (OHS) requirements for using chemicals. Alternatively, training may involve stress management techniques in a high-pressure work environment. It is well worth finding out what particular needs a company may have over and above those in the job advertisement.

4 Why is this role important to the company?

The role is important because the company wants to increase sales of its products. To do so, it thinks it needs better trained sales staff. The company will be looking for someone who can demonstrate an impact on sales through improved training.

5 What types of skills do they want and what other skills might be needed?

The company wants someone who can teach NLP. Other than that, you will need to be able to gauge whether the company's training programme is successful or not (evaluation). Other skills required are good communication skills. In this job, this involves being able to talk to groups of trainees, to produce clear training materials and to be able to write reports and present them to management. Because the company is linking the job to strategic planning, it will be important that you are able to demonstrate general business and commercial awareness. Be sure you can find your way around a balance sheet.

6 What personal qualities do they want and what other qualities might be needed?

They want someone who is 'dynamic' – meaning somebody who can motivate the sales staff and conduct interesting training courses, and generally make an enthusiastic addition. Communication and team player skills mean you need to get on well with others, speak (in public) well and write well.

7 What knowledge and training do they want and what other knowledge/training might be needed?

A degree in Psychology, Business or Commerce may be useful. Any evidence of business-related experience is probably very useful. Experience in a similar job would be good. The ability to speak a relevant language, such as French, German or Spanish, or experience working in European cultures should improve your chances.

   You can see already how, in answering these questions, we are building up a picture of the type of job on offer, and the sort of qualities the candidate should possess. Therefore, we are increasing the chances of a good fit.

You become the job detective

Below is a series of job advertisements. Have a read through each advertisement and make your own list of answers to the job interrogation questions, building your own picture of what the employer wants to see in a candidate. We have completed the first exercise for you.

Exercise 1   A worked example

ADMIN. ASSISTANT

Due to expansion, an exciting opportunity exists for a person to assist the Administration Manager in a wide variety of work such as marketing mail-outs, customer relations and all other aspects of administration. Applicants must possess good communication skills with the ability to work under pressure during peak work load times. Knowledge of Word and Excel essential. Package negotiable.

Send CV to:
Human Resources Director
Britannia Insurance
PO Box 32
London
NW1 3UL

Let's take a look at the job and examine it together. We'll start with:

1   **What don't you understand about the job ad?**

'Knowledge of Word and Excel essential.' This refers to the computer programs that you will need to know. Any job requiring significant typing or data processing work will very probably list the sort of computer programs you should be familiar with. The most common are Microsoft programs such as Word (a word-processing program) and Excel (a spreadsheet program).

'Package negotiable' means that there is no set salary for the job. You will have to negotiate it with the employer and this negotiation may also include the number of hours worked, the pension contributions and other benefits.

2   **What type of industry or company is it?**

These insurance brokers are expanding, but it is not clear whether just the one department is expanding or if the whole company is expanding. A trip to the library to look up past issues of *Euromoney* magazine will help you to work out what's happening with the company.

3   **What is the main purpose of the role?**

The main purpose of the job is administration – mail, maybe drafting correspondence, typing (using Word), filing, perhaps keeping diaries for managers, coordinating meetings, travel, and maybe working with spreadsheets (in Excel), marketing mailouts, and dealing with customers.

4   **Why is this role important to the company?**

The role is to assist the Administration Manager to process administration efficiently and effectively. Any company lives and dies on its efficiency and without an effective administration system professionally run by competent staff, profits will be seriously affected. Your role is to help the administration manager make this run smoothly.

5   **What types of skills do they want?**

Communication skills: you are likely to draft correspondence and will need to have good verbal communications to follow instructions. Time management skills: companies tend to run under time constraints, so time management skills will help you be effective in your role. Organisational skills: to help organise the company's administration you will need to be organised yourself! Customer relations: in this role you will be dealing with queries, coping with complaints and managing problems the administration manager cannot deal with. You will need to be understanding, patient and diplomatic.

6   **What types of personal qualities do they want?**

This role is clearly a support role, so reliability, punctuality, good organisational skills and attention to detail will all be highly regarded. Given that you are dealing with the public and have to work under pressure, somebody who is polite and not too hot-headed would probably be well regarded.

7   **What types of knowledge/training do they want?**

The critical training/knowledge here is in Word and Excel. Because the advertisement does not specify a level of expertise, it is fair here to assume that you will need to be reasonably proficient in both. You will need to know what the programs do, how to produce standard documents in both packages, and how to print them out or otherwise present them. You might need to become very proficient in one or both of these packages.

Here is your chance to find out if you are a Sherlock Holmes or an Inspector Clouseau. Now try examining some ads yourself. All you have to do is analyse three advertisements using our Seven Job Interrogation Questions. Use the approach we took in the last exercise as a framework, and try to be as concise as possible without missing out on anything important. You can then compare your answers with the experts' answers that follow. At the end, add up your scores to see how you went. Here is the first ad, and good luck!

Exercise 2

COMPUTER ANALYST/PROGRAMMER

An outstanding opportunity exists to join our leading edge Software Consultancy as an Analyst Programmer using the latest client/server technology. We are looking for creative and innovative thinkers who have a strong desire to be the best they can be in an environment that offers vast opportunities and rewards to dedicated and determined staff. You will be working and/or be trained alongside some of the best software developers in the field. Experience in Visual Basic, Access, SQL Server, and Internet development with tertiary qualifications would be highly regarded. If you are ambitious and have an enthusiastic personality, you are ideal for these challenging and exciting roles.

Top salary and remuneration, bonuses and incentives, with UK and/or international travel opportunities on offer to the right applicant/s.

Send CV to:
Human Resources Director
Softly Softly Ltd
Lock Hill St
Sheffield, S. Yorks
SH21 9PT

My analysis is…

1 **Check of terminology**

_____

_____

_____

2 **Type of industry/company**

_____

_____

_____

_____

3 **Main purpose of the job**

_____

_____

_____

4   Importance of the role to the company

_____

_____

_____

5   Skills wanted

_____

_____

_____

6   Personal qualities wanted

_____

_____

_____

7   Knowledge/training wanted

_____

_____

_____

Exercise 2   The experts' analysis

1   Check of terminology

Visual Basic, Access and SQL Server are technical computing terms you need to look up and understand.

2   Type of industry/company

Software consultancy.

3   Main purpose of the job

Software development using client/server technology. In this case, you would probably have to liaise with clients and come up with solutions to their software problems. This would often involve writing special programs for the clients using the computer languages listed in the ad, such as Visual Basic or Access.

4   Importance of the role to the company

'Creative and innovative thinkers' – the company is looking for people who can think outside the box in developing new software products. In other words, you should be good at being able to write computer programs that can do the tasks required by the client. Your ability to deliver programs that not only work well but address the client's needs is probably of central importance to the company.

5   Skills required

Ability to develop new software products using Visual Basic, Access, SQL Server, and the Internet.

6   Personal qualities

Creative, innovative, ambitious, dedicated, determined (tenacious?), enthusiastic. All these personal qualities suggest somebody who is good at solving the problems that clients have. This may involve coming up with different solutions for every client rather than just trying to apply the same solution to every problem. This is the 'innovative' and 'creative' part. The need for dedication and determination suggests that you need to be able to see a problem through until it is solved and not give up too easily. 'Enthusiasm' probably suggests that they are looking for somebody who relishes problem-solving.

7   Knowledge/training

The knowledge and training required are reasonably clearly stated. You must be able to use the computer programs they mention to a high standard. Tertiary qualifications seem to be valued, too.

Exercise 3

SALES REPRESENTATIVES

Deci Co. in Glasgow requires Sales Representatives to expand their sales to corporate clients. While experience in the printing industry is not essential, a proven sales and service ability in the above market would be a clear advantage. You should be highly motivated and focused on building a client base. You understand that success comes from building relationships with customers and tenaciously developing and promoting printing solutions to a wide industry client base. This position suits a practical results-driven achiever who seeks an attractive remuneration package.

Send CV to:
Douglas Giles
Giles Recruitment
PO Box 73
Glasgow
G73 2PU

My analysis is…

1 Check of terminology

_____

_____

_____

2 Type of industry/company

_____

_____

_____

3 Main purpose of the job

_____

_____

_____

4 Importance of the role to the company

_____

_____

_____

5 Skills wanted

_____

_____

_____

6   **Personal qualities wanted**

_____

_____

_____

7   **Knowledge/training wanted**

_____

_____

_____

Exercise 3   The experts' analysis

1   Check of terminology

There is little or no jargon here. The main issue would be to ensure that you understand what they mean by 'corporate clients'. (It probably means big business, but may just refer to the fact that you are selling to other companies and not to the public.)

2   Type of industry/company

Deci Co. printing products and services. What services and products do they offer? How can you find out? Call the company for a brochure. Look them up in the Yellow Pages. Search the web – use the web-based Yellow Pages (www.yell.com) and see what classification the company is listed under. Do you have any friends who might have an idea – people working in the business, or even people who work near the company's address in Sheffield?

3   Main purpose of the job

Selling printing products and providing services to corporate clients. This will probably involve persuading clients to use your company to print all their brochures, stationery or whatever else the company offers.

4   **Importance of the role to the company**

Expanding sales via building and servicing a new client base. The sales position is a crucial one for many companies, because without clients there is no business.

5   **Skills required**

The sorts of skills required will include:

- selling skills – securing new clients

- customer service – looking after existing clients

- problem-solving – identifying opportunities for new clients.

6   **Personal qualities**

These will include: highly motivated, tenacious, results-driven and achievement-orientated. These skills are important because sales staff are often paid a high proportion of their salary as commission on the sales that they achieve. Consequently you need to be the type of person who will go looking for new opportunities (motivated), be prepared to bounce back quickly when a client says no initially (tenacious) and have a need to achieve goals or meet sales targets (achievement-orientated).

7   **Knowledge/training**

Knowledge of the printing industry would be useful because it will mean you will understand the products, services and technology, know who your competitors are, who are the most likely good clients and so on. Knowledge of strategies to build a client base would also be extremely useful. This might be a good existing network of contacts who may turn into future clients, or experience of building up a network of clients in a previous job.

Exercise 4

GENERAL MANAGER – TECHNOLOGY

Our client, a national leading retailer, is seeking a General Manager to lead their business in a period of strong growth here in the UK and overseas.

The role

Principally the role will focus on developing a strategic IT plan that supports business objectives and future system requirements. There is a need to review and evaluate existing hardware/software and to manage a small support team.

The person

You are a business manager first and foremost who understands the retail industry. You have a thorough understanding of information technology, including current and future directions across the Internet/Intranet and Extranet. You possess strong people management skills and appreciate the importance of getting the best out of your staff. You have exceptional presentation skills and can tailor content to suit a broad audience. Excellent written presentation skills are required to communicate organisational needs and persuade senior management to implement system changes. This is an excellent opportunity for a successful individual to join a rapidly developing organisation and to make an impact on its future direction.

Send CV to:
Claudia Joy
Claudia Joy Ltd
PO Box 7
London WC1E 2PL

My analysis is…

1   Check of terminology

_____

_____

_____

2   Type of industry/company

_____

_____

_____

3   Main purpose of the job

_____

_____

_____

4   Importance of the role to the company

_____

_____

_____

5   Skills wanted

_____

_____

_____

6   Personal qualities wanted

_____

_____

_____

7   Knowledge/training wanted

_____

_____

_____

Exercise 4   The experts' analysis

1   Check of terminology

'IT' stands for Information Technology, which refers to electronic devices and systems that manage and share information, such as computers and networks, word processors, faxes, the Internet, email, even mobile phones. Internet, Intranet, Extranet refer to the different systems that link computers together to share information either globally (Internet), within the company (Intranet) or within a company but extending around the world (Extranet).

2   Type of industry/company

Leading national retailer: the company sells products to consumers (and possibly may manufacture them too).

3 Main purpose of the job

Managing the development and implementation of a strategic IT plan. Making sure the company has in place an IT system that can deal adequately with all the computing and communication needs of the company now and in the foreseeable future.

4 Importance of the role to the company

Providing IT solutions that are aligned with current business needs and anticipated future IT requirements is very important. There are some sorry tales around about companies having to scrap their new computer systems because they found them to be inadequate to do the job required of them. Of course such blunders are not cheap to fix.

5 Skills required

The sorts of skills required are listed below:

- leadership – implementing change
- strategic business planning
- decision-making
- people management – managing a small support team
- performance management – keeping the team's performance at the appropriate level
- presentation skills – oral and written.

6 Personal qualities

A persuasive and decisive person would probably do well here. The emphasis is on being good at getting the rest of the team working effectively and being good at taking decisions. The last point may sound strange but managers who are unable to decide between one of several options can cause tremendous problems at work, because while they are pre-varicating, nothing productive gets done!

7 Knowledge/training

The sorts of skills that would be useful include:

- knowledge of the retail industry
- business management

- IT (Internet, Intranet, Extranet)
- change management techniques.

How did you score?

Now you have analysed the sample ads, and compared your answers to those offered by our team of experts, you can find out how many points you've scored to assess how well you read the ads.

Give yourself two points each time your answer agrees with the experts. Total up your score for each job ad and look up your score using our chart below.

Scoring chart

0–8 points   Inspector Clouseau – yikes! Best to go back and start again. Writing a CV that addresses only a couple of key points is likely to get it thrown out with the rest. It may be the reason you've missed out getting shortlisted previously.

10–30 points   Dr Watson – still some work to do but you're almost halfway there. What did you miss? Go back and check the sections you scored most poorly on.

32–42 points   Sherlock Holmes – congratulations! The closer you scored to 42, the better chance you have of getting shortlisted. But be careful! In some cases, failing to identify the importance of some fundamentals like industry knowledge can still result in an almost perfect CV being rejected.

If at this stage you were unable to answer some of the questions clearly, then maybe it is because you need extra information. The following chapters describe some of the sources in more detail – so you know what you should be looking for…

5 Job descriptions

In this chapter, you will learn:

■ what a job description looks like

■ to avoid being intimidated by the qualities that are apparently demanded by a job description.

Job descriptions are another very important source of information about a job. A job description is often provided when you contact a company asking for further details. Sometimes an employer will request that you phone to collect a job description before you apply for a job. Sometimes a job description will be on hand as part of the company's normal human resources documentation. In essence, it is a longer version of the job advertisement. Some job descriptions also go into greater detail about the company and its history. In analysing job descriptions, you should ask the same seven questions as you did with the job advertisement. Here is a sample job description.

General manager
(project development)

The company (Bright & Earl Ltd)

Bright & Earl provide integrated materials, handling and distribution services for a broad and diverse client base throughout the UK. They are active in the marketplace, identifying new opportunities and providing a broad range of solutions to a diverse group of potential new clients.

The General Manager (Project Development) will play a significant role in business development, as does the General Manager (Business Development). To meet ongoing growth and the demands of project management, Bright & Earl have created the role of General Manager (Project Development), a role planned to play an integral part in the ongoing upgrading and development of the Group.

The Role

Bright & Earl are currently constructing a new facility in the North East. In the next 12 months, four sites are targeted for upgrade evaluation, with a further 16 sites across the UK targeted for evaluation of handling systems, with potential upgrades planned for three during that period. It is expected that the General Manager (Project Development) will bring exceptional Project Management, Logistics Management and Business Management skills to the Group and will be able to add value to the team, supporting the development of systems and solutions for targeted clients in the business development process, translating these into operational plans and taking into consideration all elements in the establishment of a new distribution centre from siting to construction, layout, systems, computer hardware and software, rolling stock, staffing levels, communication and administration.

The accountabilities of the role are as follows:

- identification of specific projects within existing operations, to prioritise resources in the formulation of action plans
- maintenance of project teams at required levels of skill to ensure projects are professionally managed
- establishment of detailed project plans specific to existing identified projects to manage the projects according to plan

Need to claim benefit?
Are you of working age?

There's now a new way to claim benefit.

On 24th March Jobcentre Plus offices will open in this area. If you need to claim benefit the first step is to call Jobcentre Plus.

Phone: 0845 609 3013

This is a new phone service for anyone of working age who wants to claim benefit.

- Lines are open from 8.30am to 6pm, Monday to Friday.
- Calls are charged at local rates.

We have a textphone if you are deaf, hard of hearing, or have speech difficulties.
The number is 0845 602 5015.

This new service applies if you live in one of the following postcode areas.
M14, M22 and M23

jobcentreplus

www.jobcentreplus.gov.uk

Leaflet PFL5Rush/Wyth
13th Mar 03

Part of the Department for Work and Pensions

Jobcentre Plus is here to help you find work if you are able and to give you support if you are not.

When you contact us, the person you speak to will take your details. If you are ready to start work now, they will look for suitable jobs for you.

If you need to make a claim for benefit, they will send you the forms you need.

They will also arrange a meeting with a personal adviser for you in a Jobcentre Plus office within four working days.

You must take part in a meeting and give us some basic information about your circumstances. You will not usually be able to get benefit if you do not.

To help us deal with your call quickly and efficiently, please have the following information to hand when you contact us.

We will ask you for your:
- name
- address
- date of birth
- marital status
- National Insurance number
- partner's details (if appropriate)
- dependants' details (if appropriate)
- preferred type of work
- contact phone number
- recent work history.

jobcentreplus

Part of the Department
for Work and Pensions

The services offered by the Jobcentre Plus offices are available in a number of areas across the country where the new style office has replaced the Jobcentre or social security office.

If you are not sure if you live in a Jobcentre Plus area, please get in touch.

www.jobcentreplus.gov.uk

7459

Crystal Mark

Clarity
approved by
Plain English Campaign

- management of specific projects to identify project plans to ensure projects are delivered on time

- establishment of project plans for all new business projects and managing of projects in line with the plans to ensure new business is implemented with maximum customer satisfaction

- the development and fostering of client relationships in the implementation of projects to maximise customer satisfaction

- the establishment of projects in line with the Bright & Earl established standards of quality, excellence and provision of appropriate technological solutions.

The General Manager (Project Development) will become a member of a strong management executive, with the bulk of the team being in their early to mid-30s, reporting to a General Manager who, although having an open door policy, expects his general management to operate independently and liaise with him on a needs basis. With the establishment of Project Development as a key function within the organisation, the Group General Manager has planned a restructure of some areas of the operation, with three key provisionals being transferred to a new Project Development Team. It is expected that the new General Manager (Project Development) will be able to build and motivate this newly formed division to provide specialist support at all phases of the development chain.

Selection criteria

Experience

It is expected that the successful applicant will have Project Management experience and General Management experience and will have operated in a role at a similar level for a minimum of eight years. They will have moved into this role through a career in Mechanical/Civil Engineering or Project Management within the construction industry, transport industry, warehousing and logistics within a major fast-moving consumer goods organisation, retail, fast food, banking or petrochemicals. Importantly, the successful applicant will be able to lay claim to a track record of delivery of projects on time and within budget.

The position description highlights the skills needed in this role as knowledge and experience in strategic planning and analysis, as well as:

- project management skills

- leadership and communication skills

- financial analysis and management accounting skills

- understanding and experience of CSI (continuous service improvement)

- process reengineering and benchmarking

- operational management of the field of activity

- a grasp of the core business disciplines needed for operational success

- an understanding of the ER (Employee Relations) environment and the options and process available for enterprise bargaining

- basic familiarity with ER Policy

- understanding of Commercial Law as it relates to fixing contracts, entering leases and submitting tenders

- understanding of the broader regulatory environment as it affects occupational health, workers' compensation, taxation, management and public liability.

Educational background

The successful applicant will have tertiary qualifications in a business or engineering discipline.

Personal qualities

The successful applicant will possess the following qualities:

- strategic thinking

- consummate business judgement

- the ability to influence others

- relationship management skills

- team leadership skills

- excellent listening and communication skills

- initiative

- an achievement orientation.

sample job description

In short, Bright & Earl expect an individual with innovation and vision, who can lead people effectively.

The successful applicant will have broad exposure to a diverse group of clients and suppliers and will be expected to operate effectively at all levels. It is expected that this individual will develop an awareness and knowledge of all elements affecting Bright & Earl's business operations and be able to add value to the total executive.

Employment conditions

Salary

A base salary will be negotiated in the vicinity of £40,000 per annum. Bright & Earl also offer significant incentive plans, with this position attracting a 21% bonus potential with 7% leveraged against personal contribution, 7% against project management and 7% against company results.

Other

A fully maintained car, a mobile phone and other standard benefits apply.

Searching for even more description

If a company is big enough, there may be information available in the media. This may be found in the business sections of papers, or on the Internet. Sometimes companies will be in the papers for negative reasons such as industrial unrest, injuries or discrimination cases. While the media may give only a partial view of the company, you might get some really valuable information, too.

The Internet is becoming a particularly important source of information. Many companies now have home pages on the web that will tell you a lot about them.

Company home pages can be searched for on the web using standard search engines such as Alta Vista, Yahoo! and Excite. When searching, try a variety of key words such as 'British Telecom' or 'Telecommunications Companies'. In Part 4, we provide a list of useful job-related links.

Many large-scale companies decide to subcontract their recruiting to specialist management consulting firms such as PricewaterhouseCoopers, Accenture, and Saville & Holdsworth. These firms all have home pages and within their pages there may well be links to their clients' home pages. Try looking on the web pages of the companies that place recruitment advertisements (such as Stepstone and Monster Board). The Internet is also becoming an increasingly popular medium to advertise jobs, and for people to submit their CVs. More information on using the Internet can be found in Part 4 of this book.

Finally, there are always people out there happy to pass on their opinions with little regard to how accurate they may be. We've all met the sort: 'Oh, I wouldn't work for them, they want your soul', or 'You know they invest in military hardware', or 'The boss is a drunk – it's well known', or 'They sell cigarettes to children'. Try to get as much objective evidence as possible about prospective employers. If people pass on these sorts of comments, ask them to justify what they say, or where they heard it. If they cannot come up with anything more credible than 'Everyone knows that!', or 'a friend of my brother', we suggest you disregard it.

They must want Superman!

Having read all these ads and job descriptions, you could be forgiven for thinking that companies are looking for extraordinary skills and abilities in their employees. It is only human nature – after all, if you were the employer, wouldn't you be looking for the best possible employees? However, do not be put off by the over-the-top language often used. Behind all of the bluster you have probably got all the qualities they are looking for.

Job ads often sound as though they are looking for a superhuman candidate! Don't be too easily put off from applying. If you are not in the game, you cannot win it.

Remember that your aim, as a job detective analysing job advertisements, is to try to work out what the ideal candidate or 'prime suspect' might look like. If the person you come up with could not possibly exist (no one is that perfect!) you have probably gone wrong somewhere. Go back and see where you might have exaggerated the required attributes, or where the employer might be being unrealistic.

When you have answered all these questions, you should have a much clearer picture of what it is that the company wants. It is now that you can form your plan of attack.

6 Do you fit the job?

In this chapter, you will learn how to:

■ make a list of your career milestones

■ maximise your achievements

■ tailor your achievements to the job.

Applying for a job can be very competitive, especially if the company has a good reputation, or the position is particularly exciting – both things you are looking for in a new job. It doesn't pay to over-estimate your skills beyond your abilities, but it also seriously disadvantages you if you are overly negative. It constantly amazes recruiters when they receive, all too commonly, covering letters that begin: 'Dear Sir, First of all can I point out that I don't have the required experience, but...'

Of course, nobody likes to appear big-headed, and it can be hard to describe your own abilities and not feel this way.

You see it's awfully hard to talk or write about your own stuff because if it is any good you yourself know about how good it is – but if you say so yourself you feel like a shit.

Ernest Hemingway

The point is that a potential employer wants to know what you can do, and playing down genuine abilities will not present you in the proper light.

Who are you?

Now you've painted the picture of the ideal candidate in the previous chapters, how do you go about listing your skills? Here are our tips to help you describe yourself.

When it comes to describing themselves, many people forget potentially vital details, or think that some achievements are probably irrelevant to their CV. Then again, there are some people who play down their achievements. Finally, there are those people who just cannot see that 'played in the under-sevens soccer team' is not as important as 'was elected as Prime Minister'.

In our research we found that those candidate CVs that were focused on outcomes and achievements were more likely to be shortlisted by recruiters than CVs that described the duties and responsibilities of each previous job.

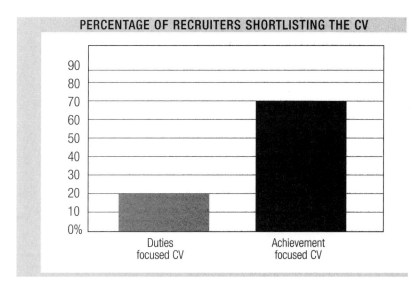

Figure 3   What is the most successful focus for your CV?

The four most common faults here are:

- forgetting some potentially impressive achievements
- thinking some achievements are not relevant
- playing down your achievements
- including every boring irrelevant detail.

You will be saying to yourself, 'Hang on, they are telling me not to exclude relevant stuff and in the next breath they are saying do not include irrelevant material. That's really helpful!'

We will introduce you to some exercises that will assist you in determining what is important and what is not.

First of all you need a list of your past activities and your achievements. We suggest that to ensure you do not omit anything by accident, you should try to list your past in as much detail as possible. At this stage do not attempt to decide whether the information is relevant or not.

We have developed some forms to help you get all the relevant details down in some order. Some people may find it easier to jot things down as they come to them which is just fine. But you may wish to put all the information onto our templates when you have finished.

Building a personal history

Divide your life into the following sections where applicable:

Stage of life	Use this template
Secondary school (typically 11 to 16 or 18 years old)	Template 1
Vocational training (16 – 22 years old)	Template 1
University (usually 18 – 21 years old)	Template 1
Any postgraduate training (typically in your 20s)	Template 1
Jobs held in the first 5 years after completing your training/education (between 20 and 30 years)	Template 2
Jobs held in your 30s	Template 2
Jobs held in your 40s	Template 2
Jobs held in your 50s and so on	Template 2
Life achievements/awards/community work/sports and hobbies	Template 3

Of course, many career histories will vary from the one shown. Here are a couple of other models.

For people without formal qualifications:

- jobs held between 15 and 20
- jobs held 20 – 30
- jobs held 30 – 40
- jobs held 40 – 50 and later

you should use Templates 2 and 3.

For people who joined the workforce later in life:

- what you did before starting training/joining the workforce
- any training
- first 5 years of work
- next 10 years
- the next 10 years, and so on

you should use all three templates, but it may be that Template 3 (the Life template) could be the most important.

You can see the general pattern we are suggesting is to divide up your life into sections which you might think of as:

- early work and training
- early jobs post-training
- mid-career jobs
- later career jobs.

When you have settled on a way of dividing up your life that suits you, use our templates to guide the process.

Template 1: Training template

For each place you did any training, complete the following details.

Secondary/ Tertiary	St Custards	Dates attended		From 1979	To 1985
Subjects studied	Results	Teams or clubs	Achievements		
Latin	C	Basketball club	I played in the cup-winning team in 1981. I captained the team in 1983 and we came second out of 20 teams.		
Home Economics	A				
Sports	D				
English	B				
Maths	C				
Spanish	U				
Geography	D				

Template 2: Jobs template

Employer Name and Address	Old Joe Pigtail And Associates 2 Railway Cuttings East Cheam Trumpton-On-Peas		Dates attended	From 1987	To 1991
Reason for leaving		To get broader experience with mega media international			

Job title	Dates	Key duties	Achievements/promotions
Junior Accounts Consultant	1987–88	Assisting Accounts Consultant	I was the first employee to be promoted to Accounts Consultant within one year, and also the youngest person to have held that position in the company's history
		Analysing sales figures	I redesigned the client reports to provide a clearer picture of year-on-year progress
Accounts Consultant	1988–91	Preparing client monthly reports on sales and promotions activities	

Training undertaken	Instructor/ organisation	Date	Description	What I learned
Effective management	Lars Toeplast Peak Managers Blue Mountains	1991	Wilderness course on team work and delegation	Taught me to set clear goals and listen to others in a group

Template 3: Life template

Activity	Dates	Description	Achievements/ personal development	Possible relevance to job
Community work	1990 to date	Bookkeeping for local branch of Oxfam	Satisfaction of giving something back to local community	Shows energy to use my accounts skills outside of normal areas
Hobbies/ interests	1992 to date	Breeding pedigree Welsh Springer Spaniels	Won best of breed, best overall at County Show	To be a breeder requires responsibility/ commitment and maturity
Sports	1979 to date	Basketball, at school, and now for the Randwick Ragers	Social life, helps keep me fit	Helps me be a team player Reduces stress
Other	1994	On the organising committee of the Festival of Food, a two-week festival aimed at promoting the local restaurants and raising awareness about diet		Good organisational skills

On Template 1 try to list the following:

- any training you undertook
- the institution
- everything you studied (the correct titles of the subjects)
- the results you got in each subject
- the overall result
- how that training was/could be useful to you in your work.

It is worth mentioning here that one of the most frequent difficulties for people reading CVs is to work out what exactly a particular qualification or result actually means. Have a look at what we have to say about this in Chapter 8.

On Template 2 list:

- all the jobs you have held
- the name of the companies
- the title of your job
- your responsibilities
- your reason for leaving
- your achievements (which we will discuss in more detail)
- any promotions.

On Template 3, include any extracurricular activities:

- sports
- committees
- interest groups (for example, amateur drama)
- training courses (such as wine appreciation, motor mechanics)
- charitable work
- hobbies.

The following tip may seem a little harsh, but remember this is from the horse's mouth!

Do a lot with your life so that there is good, interesting material to include in a well-presented CV!

Employers talk a lot about their employees 'making a contribution' and if you can demonstrate this in your CV you will be a more attractive candidate.

The more time you spend away from passive activities like watching the television, the more likely it is that you will have positive things to say on your CV. Think for one minute how society views people who do nothing but watch television in their leisure time – they are called 'couch potatoes', or worse, and this is especially damning for younger people.

List your achievements for each part of your life

It is surprising how quickly some people can forget what they have achieved or play down their role in successes. Sometimes this is because you are not feeling too good about yourself. You may have lost your job, been unemployed for a long time, or you have been out of the workforce for a long time. You must learn to recognise the symptoms if you are playing down your achievements. It is amazing, but we have seen countless university students who hold excellent degrees and Masters or PhD degrees who say, 'But I haven't really achieved anything…'

Look closely at all the activities you have listed in each period of your life.

Now think really carefully about anything that you might have achieved during this time. It might be useful for you to dip into Chapter 8 now and have a look at our 'Gestalt Rule of Proximity'. It states that people will credit you with an achievement if you were sufficiently close to it. For example, if you were a member of a team that saw sales increase 20 per cent annually, you should claim it as an achievement, even if you can't say for sure exactly how much of that outcome was directly related to your efforts.

Achievements and facts – a balancing act

If you look at our templates, you will see that they are divided roughly down the middle. On the left-hand side are the dates and jobs and hobbies. On the right-hand side we have the achievements, the promotions, the personal development.

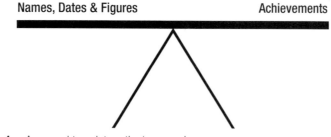

Figure 4 A general template – the 'see-saw'

Strike a balance on the information side.

It is our experience that people are great at loading the left-hand side of the see-saw while they tend to forget the right-hand side. Why is this?

Some reasons why people focus on 'names, dates and figures' are:

- they are easier to remember

- people are taught to be modest

- names, dates and figures are easier to confirm

- some people get lazy, letting the names and dates speak for them

- writing them out doesn't take much thinking.

We believe very strongly that achievements are extremely important. You can see from Figure 4 that excluding achievements will lead to an unbalanced CV. This leads us to the next two golden rules:

1   CVs exist to tell the world what you have achieved. Achievements count.
2   Everybody has achievements, some are just better at hiding them than others.

Here are some examples to help you. Check our list of possible achievements:

- promotions
- increasing sales figures
- running a project to change something in your company
- being part of a team that... (what did your team do?)
- winning an award or prize (no matter how trivial, list it)
- good results in exams or assessments
- gaining qualifications (like a degree, advanced driving qualification, heavy goods vehicle licence)
- employee of the month award
- customer service/quality awards
- outside work achievements – raising money for charity, being elected to a committee
- winning a league, a race, captaining a sports team

- long periods without absence from work (such as no sick days in three years)
- running a marathon or a fun run
- helping to paint a school/community centre
- implementation or design of systems or processes
- improving efficiencies or overhauling processes.

At the end of this chapter you should have three completed templates, and they should look well-balanced. That is, the right and left sides of them should both have plenty of information.

Well done! You now have most of the ingredients you require to build a top CV. Before we do that, in the next chapter we will consider the final ingredient – you!

7 What sort of person are you?

In this chapter, you will learn:

- what qualities employers look for

- what these qualities mean in practice

- how to check whether you possess these qualities.

Let's face it, work takes up a major part of our time, so it stands to reason that people want to work with colleagues who are pleasant and easy to get along with. If you had to choose between two equally talented workmates – one who you hated, and the other who you liked – would there really be any decision to make? Increasingly companies are becoming aware that their employees' personal habits and their work personality can not only influence the harmony of the workforce but may directly influence the quality of the work done too.

Many job ads these days list the personal qualities companies believe are important to be successful in their organisations. Many companies take this information very seriously and some will use quite sophisticated psychological tests to measure your ability to work in teams, or how quickly you might lose your temper. Other companies will invite you to join a group of other applicants to assess how well you interact with others.

Generally this sort of information is collected after reading your CV – in interviews and so on – but it is a good idea to emphasise in your CV that you will fit the company's desired 'personality'.

In this chapter, we highlight some of the most common 'psychological' traits that employers look for, explain what they mean, and demonstrate how to emphasise your strengths in these areas.

What are the most common qualities employers look for?

From a consideration of job advertisements, the following is our list of the eight most popular qualities desired:

1 Communication skills, verbal and written.
2 Team skills/team player.
3 Attention to detail.
4 Energy/dynamism/drive.
5 Initiative.
6 Ability to handle pressure.
7 Enthusiasm.
8 Leadership.

What do employers want when they ask for these qualities?

Let's consider these skills.

Communication skills

This is so common that you should assume that every job requires them – and recruiters say so too!

Assume that communication skills are important for every job and try to demonstrate them in your CV.

There is a mountain of evidence from research on employment interviews that candidates demonstrating good communication skills tend to get the highest ratings. There is no reason why you can't demonstrate these skills in your CV.

The type and degree of skill will depend on the type of job you are going for. The job might involve communicating with:

- people in your team or unit

- other units in the same organisation

- other organisations, or with the public

- special groups such as the young or elderly

- influential or senior clients such as corporate sponsors

- lawyers

- government officials

- senior managers.

What difference does it make who you communicate with? Different situations make different demands on you and you should be aware of what sort of communication you may need. While an employer might tolerate the odd gruff tone or mildly sarcastic remark in the confines of the office, a very dim view of such behaviour in front of clients will be taken.

Look at the job ad or description and try to establish who you might be communicating with the most.

The skills required may range from being able to understand and relay telephone messages clearly, to writing an extensive report or proposal, or presenting a sales pitch to customers.

Questions to ask yourself are:

- Do I speak clearly in English?

- Can I write clearly?

- Am I able to understand what people are saying to me on most occasions?

- Can I explain things to people clearly?

- So how do I demonstrate these skills on my CV?

You could draw on your work history. For instance, passing a typing test might suggest you can spell accurately, as would shorthand skills. Work as a telephonist, or as a sales representative, suggests that you can communicate verbally and effectively. Giving presentations to clients, or other public speaking experience such as toastmasters' courses, looks good.

Team skills

All this means is that you are happy and effective working in groups with other people. You are happy to work together, share information, help out team members when they are struggling. You tend to like people, and are reasonably well liked.

It sometimes seems that 'team player' is added to just about every job going without any real reason. As a general rule, it is code for saying: 'Do you get on with other people, or are you selfish and unpleasant?'

Some people think the expression 'team player' refers to membership of sporting teams. Generally this is not the case, and it is better to use examples of your team skills drawn from work experience. Of course, if you cannot think of any convincing examples from work, then you might consider using some limited example from your hobbies.

Attention to detail

Many jobs request this skill. Just because this quality is not included in an advertisement, do not assume it is not important. Making silly mistakes in some jobs such as an accounts clerk, where large sums of money may be involved, can lead to very expensive outcomes!

In a study we conducted, where we deliberately included spelling mistakes on some CVs but not on others, we found that even one error reduced the chance of the candidate being shortlisted by between 30 and 45 per cent. Think about it – just a minor error can reduce your chances of being interviewed by almost half!

Spelling errors and typos, bad grammar and poor phrasing were some of the most frequently mentioned problems with CVs by the recruiters we interviewed. Here are just a few of their tips on the subject.

Make sure there are no spelling mistakes. Use the spellchecker. Ensure your grammar and punctuation are correct.

If you are going to claim that you have good attention to detail, then demonstrate it on your CV by making sure it is completely free of mistakes. The most obvious lapse in attention to detail is spelling. How important is accurate spelling and grammar? We found that even one minor grammatical error on a CV resulted in dramatically lower ratings of the candidate. It is essential that all spelling and grammar are correct.

One recent example of a CV we saw from a student read: 'I have excellent attention to deatail'! Not only does this sentence undermine itself, it sends out warning signs – what other weaknesses does this candidate have?

Energy, dynamism, enthusiasm, drive and initiative

Nobody wants to employ somebody who slumps in their seat, seems to take for ever to carry out the most trivial tasks and sighs deeply every time they are asked to do something.

The organisation looking for the above qualities is looking for someone who is alert, gets on with work quickly without unnecessary complaint, and who (within reason) will find solutions to problems rather than find problems with solutions.

You are only human, so it is okay to feel lousy from time to time – there is nothing more irritating or downright suspect than the person who is always ecstatically happy. Do remember though that the CV is not the place for a display of negativity!

Ability to handle pressure

Pressure varies from job to job, but the request for this ability is an indication that things might get very busy from time to time. For example, work in a fire brigade or with the police force, where lapses of concentration or failures of nerve have potentially fatal outcomes! What the employer wants to see is evidence that you will respond to the challenge and perhaps work faster or longer hours on occasion to meet deadlines or reduce the backlog. What they are saying is they do not expect you to lose your temper or take sick leave at the first sign of pressure.

Pressure in some jobs will be immediate, such as a long queue of irritated customers. Or it could be longer-term stress, such as the pressure to build The Dome in time!

Leadership

Leadership is one of those qualities that tend to get thrown into a job ad without much justification. For a start, nobody can agree what makes a good leader. However, if you can demonstrate that you managed a team of people successfully, either by length of time in the position (this says that if you were not a good leader you would have been moved on quickly) or by tasks achieved by a group under your management, this may be the sort of thing the employer is looking for. Equally, being elected to a chairperson's role or similar would suggest that you command the confidence of others. Be careful not to confuse strong mindedness with leadership. The person who charges off from the social group in one direction, only to see the rest of the group subsequently set off in another direction, is demonstrating their hot-headedness, and not leadership.

How do you rate against the list of important skills?

Here are a few questions that might help you think about these skills in relation to yourself. Use these questions to trigger ideas about your personal qualities.

■ Do you tend to get details right more often than not, or do you find details irritating?

■ Do you prefer working in a team of people, or on your own?

■ Do you like to be a leader, or a team member?

■ Are you punctual for work?

■ Would you say you are outgoing, like meeting people and going to parties, or do you prefer your own company, or just a few trusted friends?

■ Do you tend to be cheerful and positive, or do you easily get depressed?

■ When people make a lot of demands on you, do you tend to remain calm, or do you find yourself losing your temper?

All of the above questions are commonly asked of candidates by employers because they are regarded as important qualities in successful employees. You may be thinking that to any or all of those questions your answer is 'Sometimes yes, sometimes no', or 'It depends', or 'It is not as simple as that'. That is a perfectly reasonable response. The point is, if these are the qualities sought by employers, the more you can demonstrate them through deeds, the better.

Exercising your skills

The following exercises should help you address these 'personality require-ments' of employers more easily.

Communication skills

List the people or group of people you commonly communicate with. Next to each person or group of people write down how you communicate. Is it face-to-face, in writing, or on the phone? What is your presentation style? Then write down how you know that what you're communicating has been successful. Take a look at our example, then try to fill out the table yourself.

Exercise 1

WHO	WHAT	SUCCESS?
Managing director	Face-to-face question	Body language, no clarification needed
Unit leader	Presentation of monthly reports	Performance appraisal requested to coach others

Team work and leadership

List examples of your ability to get on well with co-workers. Here are a few examples to guide you:

- 'The restructure motivated my new team, and we all took on extra duties to ensure that we accomplished our goals, which we actually exceeded every month.'

- 'Five of us were assigned to investigate why our customer service ratings were down. We divided the tasks up into different product areas, and decided on weekly team meetings. We soon discovered that there were some common problems, and our recommendations when implemented proved very popular.'

- 'I took on a departed colleague's duties to ensure a smooth service before a replacement was recruited for our team.'

- 'I was voted most popular employee twice last year.'

Remember, many jobs will be fairly clear whether they want a leader or a team member (or both). Looking like a leader when a team member is called for will have recruiters thinking this person will not take direction and will question decisions. Equally, if a leader is required, looking too much like 'one of the boys' might be interpreted as being a poor leader.

The following are some sample statements showing leadership:

- 'I reorganised the way payments were processed. This involved re-assigning several staff, some job enlargement and the redundancy of three staff members.'

- 'Under my management, the group has shown record profits in the past eight quarters.'

Statements showing team membership are similar to those suggesting good relations with colleagues.

Try writing your own statements to show you are outgoing, like meeting people, going to parties, or that you prefer your own company or that of just a few trusted friends. Our examples follow:

- 'I enjoy public speaking.'

- 'I am the staff social representative.'

- 'I enjoy dealing with my customers.'

- 'I enjoyed my five years in sales.'

There are few jobs that would openly seek people who are not outgoing, but they do exist. Any job where contact with other employees or the public is not frequent would be a case in point. Such jobs include machine operators, back-room processing jobs or jobs where people are out 'on the road' alone like truck drivers, or people working from home. Inadvertent statements that may make you look a little anti-social would be:

- 'I have learned to be very self-reliant.'
- 'I worked in sole practice for 20 years.'
- 'I enjoy the challenge of myself against the elements on orienteering holidays.'

Attention to detail

List work tasks or preferably results where your attention to detail has been demonstrated. For example:

- 'I have never had documents I have typed sent back to me with factual or grammatical errors in them.'
- 'During my time in this post, I reduced the amount of internal mail that was incorrectly addressed by more than 30 per cent.'

Energy, enthusiasm and initiative

Try writing your own statements after reading these samples:

- 'My project required me to identify better ways of doing things in the Accounts department to increase productivity and customer satisfaction. Mustering the talent of our Finance department, I solicited employee ideas and persuaded Management to award the best idea a £500 incentive. These ideas resulted in savings of over £500,000 to the company.'
- 'I was given the task of reorganising client files to better improve storage and retrieval. Although this was an area in which I had limited experience, I contacted my colleagues in other parts of the company and by sharing ideas with them and working long hours I implemented a new system within two weeks (three weeks earlier than my manager had expected).'

Pressure

Statements that show your calm temperament, or ability to handle pressure, might look like this:

- 'My current role regularly involves having to produce briefing reports at extremely short notice. It is satisfying to get the job done against apparently impossible odds.'

- 'A key skill is my ability to calm down angry passengers whose flights have been delayed.'

If there was a time when a job had to be finished by a deadline and you worked overnight or over the weekend to complete it, then write down the details next to the relevant job on your life history.

Finally, reflect on the places you have worked, the times you have worked (such as nightshifts or overtime) and the bosses you have worked for. Are there any things that stand out as particularly good or bad?

Where wouldn't you work?

Now is the time to make a list of things you will not put up with in the workplace. To do this, make three lists with the following headings:

1   I will never work in a place that...

2   I will only put up with... if it happens very rarely.

3   I would prefer not to work in a place that... but I know I can cope if necessary.

The things you might put on this list include:

- bad-tempered boss
- lots of people smoking
- few people of my gender or ethnic background at work
- premises in the middle of town
- premises out of town
- no car parking
- very poor safety.

Your pantry of ingredients

You should now have several templates setting out all the things that you have done over your working life, and how you see yourself. Think of this as your 'pantry' of ingredients. This is what we will use to make your tailored CV, and brings us to our next golden rule.

Take time every couple of months to update your skills and achievements list. This way you will always have an up-to-date list and you are less likely to forget your achievements over time.

Now you have all this information about yourself, you have one task left. Give all the information to somebody who knows you very well, and who you trust. Ask them 'Is this me?' and 'Is there anything I've left out?'. If you are embarrassed about showing someone else all those immodest achievements we asked you to list, blame us! We told you to do it.

You are now ready to start deciding what goes into your CV.

Before choosing a style of CV, you need to start matching your personal achievements and qualities with the job detective work you have done. You should, by this stage, have a good idea of what the job requirements are and this information should guide you in choosing which achievements and personal qualities you should include. The challenge here is different for different groups. Use our work history achievement charts on the next page to assist you in this task.

Career stage	Information to emphasise	Key challenges for your CV
School leaver	Qualifications Personality/life skills Community involvement Any work experience Your age (so people do not expect too much work experience if you are young) Hobbies	Demonstrate to an employer that you have some skills to offer (either through your qualifications or through community involvement). Demonstrate readiness to enter the workforce through responsibility, reliability and maturity.
Graduate	Qualifications Any work experience, including visits and placements as a part of your studies Awards Community involvement Personality/life skills	Show an employer that you are more than just a brainbox, that you are well rounded, are involved in things outside study, that you have not wasted the opportunities that university offers. Demonstrate evidence of responsibility, leadership, maturity and, if relevant, commercial awareness.
Early career	Qualifications Work experience Work achievements Personality Life skills	Show how you have progressed and what new skills you've learned in the workforce. Show a logical pattern in the work history that tells a story, and that this job is the logical next step.
Mid career	Work experience, especially the past five years and anything relevant to the position applied for Work achievements Positions of leadership/ responsibility	Demonstrate a period of sustained success and recognition at work. The story needs to tell of a steady (or faster) rise up the organisational ladder, or alternatively, a steady (or better) stream of achievement and recognition.

Career stage	Information to emphasise	Key challenges for your CV
Mid career	Relevant training courses, or industry qualifications Membership of professional associations	Show a broadening of your industry experience, or mastery of your chosen skill.
Late career	Leadership and management skills or mastery of a set of skills Wide experience across situations, organisations and/or countries Professional recognition of your status	Show that you can fit into the organisation and help them out from Day 1. Demonstrate a track record of success. Come across as totally sound and remove any doubts about your ability to the job with assurance.
Career change	Transferable skills, any skills or experience that may be relevant to the chosen career Any relevant skills acquired in a previous career to the one you are leaving Evidence of personal qualities such as flexibility and willingness to learn	Think about your current work experience from an outsider's perspective. Can you portray mundane skills in a new light that makes them seem relevant? Convince the recruiter that this is a considered move and a logical progression, or sensible change. Minimise the differences between you and the new job.
Re-entry to the workforce after a break	Qualifications that are still current Any activities and achievements in the time away from work Efforts to keep yourself up to date, current market knowledge Personal qualities that are relevant to the job and that show market/commercial awareness	Show that you are not completely out of touch and that you have something very valuable to offer that ideally will not cost the company a lot of time and money in developing. Demonstrate how you spent your time out of the workforce responsibly and productively. Be aware that your reasons for being out of the workforce may not be highly valued by the employer.

8 Making the perfect fit

In this chapter, you will learn:

■ what chronological, functional, hybrid and structured interview CVs look like

■ how to tailor a CV for you and the job.

How do I set out my CV?

There are several ways of writing a CV. Different approaches work for different people. The three most popular CV styles are the:

■ chronological CV

■ functional CV

■ hybrid CV.

To these three, we will add the structured interview CV.

Chronological CV

This CV is the style many people use without thinking. It lists your training and jobs in order of the dates you commenced each of them. Typically, people list their most recent training or jobs first and proceed back to the first things they did. This is called the 'reverse chronological' CV.

The components of this CV are in order:

1 Personal details.

2 Qualifications.

3 Professional development/training courses.

4 Employment history, including:

- employer
- dates of employment
- positions held
- achievements.

Here is a quick example of the chronological CV.

Bob Brown

Address:	10 Elm Ave
	London, SW2 4UL
Contact details:	(H) 020 8311 3111
	(W) 020 8222 2222

Qualifications

1983–1985	BA in Management, University of London
	Majoring in Accounting and Commercial Law

Professional development

I have attended training courses in the following:

- Consultative selling
- Analytical skills
- Negotiation
- Time management
- Business management
- Executive development programme.

Employment history

Jones Bros Ltd

Jones Bros is a large national company which owns a range of goods transportation systems. Next Day Freight provides distribution systems for a broad customer base including a range of major UK companies.

Regional Manager for Next Day Freight   3/00 to present
Reporting to the General Manager.

My major responsibilities in this position include acting as a change agent reshaping the business into a professional and profitable organisation with a strong emphasis on customer service. The bottom line responsibility of this position is a £50 million business unit employing 350 people in Sales, Administration, Operations, Marketing, Customer Service, Quality and Security.

My major achievements in this position include:

- creation and implementation of a regional business plan addressing major shortfalls in the business

- a successful merger with a £10 million business unit

- restructuring of the entire sales force

- negotiation and implementation of a new enterprise agreement

- complete management restructure

- introduction of new Management Information Systems

- negotiating the outsourcing of £2.5 million p.a. of casual labour

- coordinating the building of a major new depot facility

- implementation of a quantifiable quality improvement programme

- development of a new marketing strategy

- development of a major strategic industrial relations plan to create greater incentive for the workforce

- leading the business unit to its best profit performance.

National Petroleum Ltd

National is a major petroleum company that owns refineries nationally, as well as having a major franchise network of petrol stations.

National Distribution Network Manager   *3/95 to 2/00*

Reporting to the National Planning Manager.

In this role, I was responsible for the strategic development and network rationalisation of the wholesale distribution business worth over £80 million p.a. to company profit. I was responsible for maintaining primary trade and developing an environment for improved profit performance based on best practices, operating efficiency and optimum capital investment.

Major milestones in this role included:

- comprehensive review of the sector and development of an integrated business plan for the next century
- development of a new network process to contain the best demographic mix of distribution and marketing
- development and implementation of a merchandising-based franchise package
- implementation of a business planning process for independent distributors
- strategic business review of a £300 million subsidiary
- management of the wholesale investment budget to achieve corporate objectives
- successful rationalisation and restructuring of the distributor business to improve the return on investment.

Regional Finance Manager   *3/93 to 2/95*

Reporting to the Regional Manager.

My major responsibilities in this role were the financial performance of the dealer and distributor businesses within the area, and entailed the management of profitability, franchisee selection and administration.

Senior Reseller Area Manager   *1/91 to 2/93*

Reporting to the Wholesale Network Development Manager.

Responsible for bottom line profit, achievement of volume targets, financial management and credit control, tendering for new business and network development.

Marketing, Planning and Economics Officer   *2/89 to 12/90*

Responsible for SWOT analyses, forecasting and preparation of cost submissions.

Transport Distribution Manager   *2/88 to 1/89*

Consulting to wholesale fuel distributors.

Rundle and Smith Chartered Accountants   *1/86 to 1/88*

Team audit work for a range of companies.

Reason for leaving: to pursue a marketing career.

Interests

Swimming, tennis and bike riding, competitive squash, share dealing.

Referees

Available upon request.

Functional CV

This is a style that emphasises the skills of the individual and their achievements. It is often used when the applicant lacks formal qualifications, or their qualifications are judged obsolete or irrelevant. If you have had many different jobs with no clear pattern of progression, or a lot of gaps in your work history, some people recommend this approach. You do not, after all, want to present your career as a drunken stagger through the world of work!

Bob Brown

Address:	10 Elm Ave
	London, SW2 4UL
Contact details:	(H) 020 8311 3111
	(W) 020 8222 2222

Qualifications

1983–1985   BA in Management, University of London
Majoring in Accounting and Commercial Law

Skills, knowledge, attributes and abilities

Communication skills

In my role as Regional Manager for Next Day Freight I am required to liaise across a broad cross-section of employees. In order to keep employees abreast of company direction and anticipated changes, I implemented briefing sessions held across all shifts once a month. Here I was able to communicate directly with the staff myself and field any questions. Employee satisfaction regarding communications improved from 2.5 to 4.3 over a 12-month period.

Business management

I have a sound knowledge of business management principles. Having completed studies in Management at the University of London, I have continued to keep myself up to date with recent trends and developments by subscribing to journals and magazines. I have also attended several training courses, including the London Business School Executive Development Programme and specialist management courses. Over the past three years, I have implemented ideas gained from my knowledge to restructure our sales force, supervise the implementation of a new Management Information System and quality improvement programme.

Selling skills

As National Distribution Network Manager for National Petroleum Ltd., I was responsible for developing a merchandising-based franchise package which aimed at converting successful franchisees with other companies to National Petroleum. I developed a programme which targeted the top 100 successful franchisees and by interviewing a cross-section, identified reasons most would convert. I then developed a selling kit for representatives to use and conducted selling-skills training courses for representatives to develop better levels of skill. I dealt with the top three clients personally and all three converted. Of the remaining 97 franchisees, 70 per cent converted.

Negotiation skills

In my capacity as Regional Manager for Next Day Freight, I have been required to address numerous issues regarding workforce planning. This included outsourcing £2.5 million worth of casual labour, implementing a staff incentive programme and developing a new enterprise agreement. These represented major changes for our existing and often volatile workforce. By developing a committee (which I chaired) involving employee, management and union representatives, we have been able to successfully introduce the required changes without any lost time. Employee satisfaction with working conditions has risen from 1.8 to 4.0 over the past three years.

Tenacity

On my appointment to the position of Regional Manager Next Day Freight, I quickly identified potential cost savings in merging our business unit with our sister company's (Parcel Pick Up) business unit worth £10 million. The project to merge the two units was finally realised last month after planning and negotiations spanning more than three years. Anticipated cost savings as a result of the merger are likely to be in the vicinity of £5 billion.

Summary of employment history

3/00 to now	Jones Bros Ltd	Regional Manager Next Day Freight
3/95 to 2/00	National Petroleum Ltd	National Distribution Network Manager
3/93 to 2/95		Regional Finance Manager
1/91 to 2/93		Senior Reseller Area Manager
2/89 to 12/90		Marketing, Planning and Economics Officer
2/88 to 1/89		Transport Distribution Manager
1/86 to 1/88	Rundle and Smith Chartered Accountants	Team audit work for a range of companies. Reason for leaving: to pursue a marketing career.

Interests

Swimming, tennis and bike riding, competitive squash, share dealing.

Referees

Available upon request.

Hybrid CV

This is an increasingly popular approach that combines the best of both the chronological CV and the functional CV. A hybrid CV retains much of the fixed order of the chronological CV but there is a lot more emphasis on skills and achievements – sometimes in a separate section.

The hybrid approach is the one that we recommend to most people, in so far as it produces an excellent clear structure but requires the candidate to really think hard about their achievements and what they have to offer. Obviously there is a limit to how long your CV should be. If you decide to use a hybrid style, you may wish to leave out the detailed responsibilities section and just emphasise the skills, knowledge and abilities.

Bob Brown

Address:	10 Elm Ave
	London, SW2 4UL
Contact details:	(H) 020 8311 3111
	(W) 020 8222 2222

Qualifications

1983–1985	BA in Management, University of London
	Majoring in Accounting and Commercial Law

Professional development

I have attended training courses in the following:

- consultative selling
- analytical skills
- negotiation

- time management
- business management
- executive development programme.

Skills, knowledge, attributes and abilities

Communication skills

In my role as Regional Manager for Next Day Freight I am required to liaise across a broad cross-section of employees. In order to keep employees abreast of company direction and anticipated changes, I implemented briefing sessions held across all shifts once a month. Here I was able to communicate directly with the staff myself and field any questions. Employee satisfaction regarding communications improved from 2.5 to 4.3 over a 12-month period.

Business management

I have a sound knowledge of business management principles. Having completed studies in Management at the University of London, I have continued to keep myself up to date with recent trends and developments by subscribing to journals and magazines. I have also attended several training courses, including the London Business School Executive Development Programme and specialist management courses. Over the past three years, I have implemented ideas gained from my knowledge to restructure our sales force, supervise the implementation of a new Management Information System and quality improvement programme.

Selling skills

As National Distribution Network Manager for National Petroleum Ltd., I was responsible for developing a merchandising-based franchise package which aimed at converting successful franchisees with other companies to National Petroleum. I developed a programme which targeted the top 100 successful franchisees and by interviewing a cross-section, identified reasons most would convert. I then developed a selling kit for representatives to use and conducted selling-skills training courses for representatives to develop better levels of skill. I dealt with the top three clients personally and all three converted. Of the remaining 97 franchisees, 70 per cent converted.

Negotiation skills

In my capacity as Regional Manager for Next Day Freight I have been required to address numerous issues regarding workforce planning. This included outsourcing £2.5 million worth of casual labour, implementing a staff incentive programme and developing a new enterprise agreement. These represented major changes for our existing and often volatile workforce. By developing a committee (which I chaired) involving employee, management and union representatives, we have been able to successfully introduce the required changes without any lost time. Employee satisfaction with working conditions has risen from 1.8 to 4.0 over the past two years.

Tenacity

On my appointment to the position of Regional Manager Next Day Freight I quickly identified potential cost savings in merging our business unit with our sister company's (Parcel Pick Up) business unit worth £10 million. The project to merge the two units was finally realised last month after planning and negotiations spanning more than three years. Anticipated cost savings as a result of the merger are likely to be in the vicinity of around £5 billion.

Employment history

Jones Bros Ltd 3/00 to present

Jones Bros is a large national company which owns a range of goods transportation systems. Next Day Freight provides distribution systems for a broad customer base including a range of major UK companies.

Regional Manager for Next Day Freight

Reporting to the General Manager, my major achievements in this position include:

- creation and implementation of a regional business plan addressing major shortfalls in the business
- a successful merger with a £10 million business unit
- restructuring of the entire sales force
- negotiation and implementation of a new enterprise agreement
- complete management restructure
- introduction of new Management Information Systems
- negotiating the outsourcing of £2.5 million p.a. of casual labour
- coordinating the building of a major new depot facility
- implementation of a quantifiable quality improvement programme
- development of a new marketing strategy

- development of a major strategic industrial relations plan to create greater incentive for the workforce
- leading the business unit to its best profit performance.

National Petroleum Ltd

National Distribution Network Manager   *3/95 to 2/00*

Reporting to the National Planning Manager, my major milestones in this role included:
- a comprehensive review of the sector and development of an integrated business plan for the next century
- development of a new network process to contain the best demographic mix of distribution and marketing
- the development and implementation of a merchandising-based franchise package
- implementation of a business planning process for independent distributors
- a strategic business review of a £300 million subsidiary
- management of the wholesale investment budget to achieve corporate objectives
- successful rationalisation and restructuring of the distributor business to improve the return on investment.

Regional Finance Manager   *3/93 to 2/95*

Reporting to the Regional Manager, my major responsibilities in this role were the financial performance of the dealer and distributor businesses within the area, and entailed the management of profitability, franchisee selection and administration.

Senior Reseller Area Manager   *1/91 to 2/93*

Reporting to the Wholesale Network Development Manager.

I was responsible for bottom line profit, achievement of volume targets, financial management and credit control, tendering for new business and network development.

Marketing, Planning and Economics Officer   *2/89 to 12/90*

Responsible for SWOT analyses, forecasting and preparation of cost submissions.

Transport Distribution Manager   *2/88 to 1/89*

Consulting to wholesale fuel distributors.

Rundle and Smith Chartered Accountants   *1/86 to 1/88*

Team audit work for a range of companies. Reason for leaving: to pursue marketing career.

Interests

Swimming, tennis and bike riding, competitive squash, share dealing.

Referees

Available upon request.

The structured interview CV

This is an idea that might work for some people. In a structured interview, the job applicant is asked a series of questions in a set order. In a structured interview CV, the candidate sets out a series of questions and provides the answers to them. Increasingly, these types of questions are being asked on web-based job application forms, so setting out your CV in this manner may elicit a positive response from the recruiter. This approach emphasises skills and competencies over formal qualifications. The following questions can be used to make up a structured interview CV.

Communication skills

- What types of proposals have you written?
- What are some of the most difficult groups you've had to present to?

Business management

- How does your experience in business management match our role requirements?

Selling skills

- What has been the toughest selling assignment you have ever had?

Negotiation skills

- What do you believe are the successful outcomes of a good negotiation process?
- When have you best demonstrated your negotiation skills?

Tenacity

- Describe a project or work assignment that best demonstrates your tenacity.

Structured interview example

Let's look at our sample CV, presented as a structured interview.

Bob Brown

Address:	10 Elm Ave
	London, SW2 4UL
Contact details:	(H) 020 8311 3111
	(W) 020 8222 2222

Qualifications

1983–1985	BA in Management, University of London
	Majoring in Accounting and Commercial Law

Employers

1995–2000	National Petroleum Ltd.
2000 to present	Jones Bros Ltd (Next Day Freight)

Professional development

I have attended training courses in the following:

- consultative selling
- analytical skills
- negotiation
- time management
- business management
- executive development programme.

Skills, knowledge, attributes and abilities

Communication skills

What types of proposals have you written?

I have written a wide range of proposals, in terms of significance and audience. Proposals have included change in marketing strategy proposals for presentation to Board of Directors; Industrial Relations proposals for presentation to Board of Directors and Union representatives; a prospectus for potential franchisees; merger recommendations for presentation to our Board of Directors and to the Board of Directors of proposed merging company.

What are some of the most difficult groups you've had to present to?

Although I have had no 'difficult groups' as such, I have needed to present to some quite sceptical and cautious groups. These have included union organisers, potential franchisees and the board of directors of a company we were proposing to merge with. All groups were significant stakeholders with a lot to lose from a poor decision, and consequently there were a lot of questions to field and I was forced to think quickly. Presentations were designed to address the audiences' primary concerns in a style that they were most comfortable with. In the above examples my presentations contributed to successful outcomes in all three cases.

Business management

How does your experience in business management match our role requirements?

Over the past nine years my roles have primarily focused on business management. I have a broad background in most aspects of general management including finance, sales, marketing, distribution, business development and, most recently, human resources, in my role as Regional Manager. My experience is complemented by formal studies in Accounting and Commercial Law, demonstrating that I can successfully convert theory into practice. I have the necessary breadth and depth of experience to fulfil or exceed requirements as the Regional Manager for Overnight-Now.

Selling skills

What has been the toughest selling assignment you have ever had?

The toughest selling assignment has been converting existing successful franchisees to change to National Petroleum. Already proven to be successful with GDP Petrol, these franchisees had more to gain by converting to National Petroleum, but naturally some were sceptical. I set about finding the franchisees' most frequent source of dissatisfaction with GDP and structured a package that addressed these concerns. Since there were 100 franchisees to convert, I could not handle all of these myself. By training our representatives, 97 franchisees were approached, of which 70 per cent converted. I managed the relationship with the top three franchisees personally, and all converted.

Negotiation skills

What do you believe are the successful outcomes of a good negotiation process?

A genuine win-win result for both parties. I think it is important to go into a negotiation with a clear understanding of what I want to achieve, as well as being prepared to listen to what the other party wants. At the end of the negotiation there needs to be a set of outcomes agreed to and honoured by both parties.

When have you best demonstrated your negotiation skills?

During our enterprise agreement negotiation at Next Day Freight. Management was keen to introduce significant changes to the types of skills, shift rosters and duties performed by employees to deliver maximum workforce flexibility in our 2000 negotiations. These changes represented significant cost savings to the business as well as ensuring longer-term business viability. Without these changes, it was likely that the business would need to retrench many of its current permanent workforce and outsource functions to contractors. By creating a committee of employee, management and union representatives, we were able to successfully identify what each group wanted to achieve. All three groups reached agreement on the issues that were key to their concerns, and conceded on smaller, less important issues. There was no time lost as a result of the negotiations and employee satisfaction rose significantly.

Tenacity

How tenacious are you? Give an example that demonstrates you at your most tenacious.

Of course, I am very tenacious, as can be demonstrated by the successful merger between Next Day Freight and Parcel Pick-Up. Parcel Pick-Up was a family business passed down through three generations and was suffering badly from the high cost of its overheads and a downturn in its speciality service – small parcel delivery. I met with the then Managing Director in 2000 to discuss the possibility of a merger, and it was clear that he was not prepared to concede. It took almost a year of regular meetings and negotiations to build his confidence in our business. In 2001, we successfully merged, retaining all existing staff, combining support functions and sharing overheads.

Employment history

Jones Bros Ltd 3/2000 to present

Jones Bros is a large national company which owns a range of goods transportation systems. Next Day Freight provides distribution systems for a broad customer base including a range of major UK companies.

Regional Manager for Next Day Freight

Reporting to the General Manager. My major responsibilities in this position include acting as a change agent reshaping the business into a professional and profitable organisation with a strong emphasis on customer service. The bottom-line responsibility of this position is a £50 million business unit employing 350 people in sales, administration, operations, marketing, customer service, quality and security.

My major achievements in this position include:

- creation and implementation of a state business plan addressing major shortfalls in the business

- a successful merger with £10 million business unit

- restructuring of the entire sales force

- negotiation and implementation of a new enterprise agreement

- complete management restructure

- introduction of new Management Information Systems

- negotiating the outsourcing of £2.5 million p.a. of casual labour

- coordinating the building of a major new depot facility

- implementation of a quantifiable quality improvement programme

- development of a new marketing strategy

- development of a major strategic industrial relations plan to create greater incentive for the workforce

- leading the business unit to its best profit performance.

National Petroleum Ltd

National is a major petroleum company that owns refineries nationally, as well as having a major franchise network of petrol stations.

National Distribution Network Manager   *3/95 to 2/2000*

Reporting to the National Planning Manager.

In this role, I was responsible for the strategic development and network rationalisation of the wholesale distribution business worth over £80 million p.a. to company profit. I was responsible for maintaining primary trade and developing an environment for improved profit performance based on best practices, operating efficiency and optimum capital investment.

Major milestones in this role included:

- a comprehensive review of the sector and development of an integrated business plan for the next century
- development of a new network process to contain the best demographic mix of distribution and marketing
- the development and implementation of a merchandising-based franchise package
- implementation of a business planning process for independent distributors
- a strategic business review of a £300 million subsidiary
- management of the wholesale investment budget to achieve corporate objectives
- successful rationalisation and restructuring of the distributor business to improve the return on investment.

Regional Finance Manager   *3/1993 to 2/1995*

Reporting to the Regional Manager.

My major responsibilities in this role were the financial performance of the dealer and distributor businesses within the area, and entailed the management of profitability, franchisee selection and administration.

Senior Reseller Area Manager   *1/1991 to 2/1993*

Reporting to the Wholesale Network Development Manager.

Responsible for bottom-line profit, achievement of volume targets, financial management and credit control, tendering for new business and network development.

Marketing, Planning and Economics Officer   *2/1989 to 12/1990*

Responsible for SWOT analyses, forecasting and preparation of cost submissions.

Transport Distribution Manager   *2/1988 to 1/1989*

Consulting to wholesale fuel distributors.

Rundle and Smith Chartered Accountants   *1/1986 to 1/1988*

Team audit work for a range of companies. Reason for leaving: to pursue a marketing career.

Interests

Swimming, tennis and bike riding, competitive squash, share dealing.

Referees

Available upon request.

Which CV is for me?

Our extensive work has found that recruiters prefer CVs that look conventional. This has been found in studies throughout the world. Most recruiters are conventional people, and they have a clear idea of what they expect to see when they read a CV.

Reading a CV is a bit like walking into a restaurant – we know what to expect. In a restaurant, we know that there will be tables and a menu, that we will be asked for our order and we will have to pay for the food. We might even expect to leave a tip! Receiving an unusual CV would be like walking into the restaurant and seeing no tables or serving staff. We might work out that there is a food vending machine to use, or alternatively we might just walk out. Similarly, we might persevere with an unusual CV, or we might just reject it.

Before we look at some actual examples, we will take a look at what things you should put in your CV. The following is our list of important elements of a CV.

Use our 4-S rule – keep it **S**imple, **S**tructured, **S**uccinct and **S**ignificant.

Essential contact details

Always include your:

- full name
- home address
- telephone number
- mobile number
- fax number
- email address.

Only give contact details for places where you are prepared to be contacted by prospective employers. If receiving a call or an email at your current workplace might lead to embarrassing questions from your boss, do not give work contact details. Of course, if you want to include an email address, it is now very easy to get a free email account on the web from companies like Hotmail (www.hotmail.com).

You must put your name, address and telephone number on the first page of your CV.

Education and training

If you don't have any formal education, obviously you omit these elements and should be thinking of using the functional or the structured interview CV.
Have a look at the ideal candidate you constructed from the job ad in Chapter 4. What qualifications is our potential employer looking for? These qualifications are the ones to focus on.

Do not bore the reader by listing every qualification you have obtained – keep it to the relevant and impressive stuff.

Go through the list of qualifications you have made and determine which are relevant to the job. List these in order.

Some qualifications, like a university degree, are regarded as relevant information in most circumstances. Other qualifications, such as a first aid course, may be seen as useful for some jobs, but would look odd being listed for others.

Your age will also help you decide what to include and what to leave out. For people in their first five years of work, education is very important and should be listed in reasonable detail. After those first five years, be a bit more selective about what you use.

Some qualifications become outdated quickly, so claiming to be a computer expert on the basis of a computing degree obtained 15 years ago will not look very convincing. In this case, evidence of recent work in the field will count for a lot more.

Having said that, a degree shows evidence of critical thinking and intelligence and should not be discarded altogether.

Be clear, concise and always refer back to the job ad to ensure you're remaining relevant.

The order in which you list qualifications is normally:

- highest postgraduate qualification – Masters or PhD, the subject, and the university at which the degree was taken
- highest undergraduate qualification – the degree, the subject, and the university at which the degree was taken
- secondary school qualifications.

This point may not apply to many people at all, but should you have a PhD, bear in mind that the title of PhDs can often appear to be so obscure or trivially narrow as to detract from a great achievement. Believe us, we have heard the sniggers that sometimes accompany PhD award presentation ceremonies! If you have a very specialised title that is not going to be directly relevant to the job applied for, then stick to the subject discipline name (such as chemistry, physics, English, or psychology).

If you have a degree, it is probably not too important to go into detail about your secondary school results unless they are exceptional. If you have a degree, most employers will credit you with a certain amount of intelligence. What might be useful is to list a few subjects you covered at secondary school, to give an indication of your versatility. For instance, if you have an arts degree, it is probably worth listing 'mathematics, chemistry, statistics' or other numerate subjects studied at secondary school, as this gives an indication of rounded abilities. The opposite applies for science graduates, who might list English and history if applicable.

List any extra languages that you speak, but see our later section on bias.

If there is any special thesis topic or aspect of your studies that is particularly relevant to the job, then mention it here.

With all qualifications, do not assume that the reader will understand what they are. For instance, what do the following mean?

- HSC
- SNVQ
- GSCE
- O-level
- A-level
- cum laude
- Honours
- ACA, RIBA
- Baccalaureate
- City and Guilds
- Grade point average or GPA.

Chances are, some of the above will be a mystery to you. If you are applying for a job in the same country in which you were trained and the qualification system has not changed in the last ten years, it is safe to assume the employer will understand the meaning of your qualifications. Otherwise, do not assume anyone else will understand your qualifications – if in doubt explain what they mean.

If you gained your qualifications overseas, say what the local equivalent qualification is and, even better, get your qualifications assessed by the relevant government department. If in doubt, contact the local immigration department for assistance.

Look at the following grading systems.

You cannot be sure that 75 per cent from one course is equal to a 'B' in another. A good example comes from UK and Australian universities. In the UK, a 'First' or 'A' is often awarded for scores above 75 per cent, whereas that score in Australia is often a 'two-one' or 'B'. The educational standard is probably not too different, it is just the way people use the scales.

You can be sure that if an employer has any doubts they will tend to think the worst.

When applying for a job in another state or country, don't assume employers will understand what your qualifications mean. Explain your grades in the employer's local system.

Your work history

Go back to the lists that you have made and try to pick out what in your work history either matches the ideal candidate you have constructed, or looks impressive in its own right.

Your work history is the most 'wordy' part of the CV. This is where you have the most scope to influence the reader through your writing style, the words you use, and the way you describe yourself.

Generally list your most recent job first, and then move onto the previous one and so on. If you have a long work history with many different jobs, then we would recommend you restrict listing full details of the positions held in the past ten years. If there are some earlier jobs that are particularly relevant to the application then these should be included.

For each job you should list:

- dates (in years) of employment
- job title
- employer's name and city location if appropriate
- your responsibilities (keep it brief)
- your achievements in the job.

Tailor the CV to suit the requirements of the ad and include achievements (not just duties), because this is what will sell you.

The last point on this list is possibly one of the most important. Just providing a job description is not enough. If many applicants have similar backgrounds then the recruiter will be bored to tears and may not even read your CV. What makes you different, more employable, are all of your achievements.

In a study we conducted, recruiters were shown two CVs that were identical except that one described only duties in the job history and the other described achievements. The CV that included achievements was rated much more highly by the recruiters. They were far more impressed with the candidate.

Always emphasise your achievements in each job.

The following is a typical job history.

Employment history

Trinity Mutual Ltd

What does this company do?

Executive Director, Trinity Mutual Master Trust – 3/1998 to present

Key responsibilities include all aspects of the Master Trust, with 25 staff across four departments including marketing, client administration, systems and accounting.

President Mutual – 1984 to 1998

Any achievements?

Marketing Manager – 1996 to 1997

Key responsibilities included product development and maintenance, marketing and communications of the entire product range of the division.

Assistant General Manager, Financial Products – 1995 to 1996

As above.

Senior Investment Manager, Operations – 1991 to 1995

Key responsibilities included the day to day operations of President Funds Management and 'unusual' investments such as leveraged leases, junk bonds, etc.

Fund Manager, Life Fund and Insurance Bonds – 1990 to 1991

Key responsibilities included managing the £3.5 billion Life Fund and the £1.5 billion Insurance Bond Fund, including asset allocation, general management and 'unusual' investments.

Fund Manager, Insurance Bonds – 1987 to 1990

Key responsibilities included managing the new Insurance Bond Fund, including asset allocation, general management and 'unusual' investments.

Actuarial and investment roles – 1984 to 1987

In this period I was engaged in a number of actuarial roles and investment positions within President Mutual.

The achievement focus

Here is the same job history, but this time there is an emphasis on achievements.

Employment history

Trinity Mutual Ltd – 3/1998 to present

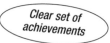
Tells you what the company does

Trinity Mutual is a major insurance agency which operates Europe-wide.

Executive Director, Trinity Mutual Master Trust – 3/1998 to present

Key responsibilities include all aspects of the Master Trust, with 25 staff across four departments including marketing, client administration, systems and accounting. Major achievements included successful relocation of the administration, accounting and systems areas from external suppliers to head office.

President Mutual Ltd – 1984 to 1998

Clear set of achievements

President Mutual is a major insurance agency which operates UK-wide.

Marketing Manager – 1996 to 1997

Key responsibilities included product development and maintenance, marketing and communications of the entire product range of the division. During this time sales rose by 14 per cent, compared with a 5 per cent rise average in the area.

Assistant General Manager, Financial Products – 1995 to 1996

As above.

Senior Investment Manager, Operations – 1991 to 1995

Key responsibilities included the day to day operations of President Funds Management and 'unusual' investments such as leveraged leases, junk bonds.

Fund Manager, Life Fund and Insurance Bonds – 1990 to 1991

Key responsibilities included managing the £3.5 billion Life Fund and the £1.5 billion Insurance Bond Fund, including asset allocation, general management and 'unusual' investments. The fund outperformed all the indexes.

Fund Manager, Insurance Bonds – 1987 to 1990

Key responsibilities included managing the new Insurance Bond Fund, including asset allocation, general management and 'unusual' investments.

Major achievements included growing the Fund from £5 million to more than £1 billion.

Actuarial and investment roles – 1984 to 1987

In this period, I was engaged in a number of actuarial roles and investment positions within President Mutual.

Turning responsibilities into achievements

What has this person achieved?

General Manager, Merchandise and Marketing

The major responsibilities in this role included:

- overall accountability for the product, merchandising and promotions for the 100 stores Europe-wide
- product sourcing
- financial control of the sales budget
- managing the team of 12 buying and merchandising staff
- ongoing liaison with state management
- control and accountability of the advertising and marketing needs of the stores.

What would you look for? Where might there be places where achievements could be emphasised?

The first thing to catch the eye is the overall accountability for 100 stores. Can the applicant point to any financial improvements in the stores' performance? What about the sourcing of the products – any reduction in costs there, or sources of novel products?

The role is a coordinating one – is there any evidence of achievements in organising the systems the applicant controls? Did the applicant introduce any new marketing strategies or just carry on where their predecessor left off? (That is, did they show initiative?)

The above description could be enhanced by referring directly to achievements that answer these questions. Remember, the CV is supposed to answer questions, not raise them in the minds of the recruiter. The improved version is below.

General Manager, Merchandise and Marketing

The major responsibilities in this role included:

- overall accountability for the product, merchandising and promotions for the 100 stores Europe-wide
- product sourcing
- financial control of the sales budget
- managing the team of 12 buying and merchandising staff
- ongoing liaison with state management
- control and accountability of the advertising and marketing needs of the stores.

Major achievements included:

- restructure of the buying department, resulting in increased productivity and lower costs
- changes to the supply chain, resulting in a 4 per cent increase in margins
- development of reporting systems, resulting in enhanced financial planning
- introduction of new offshore merchandise resources
- development and implementation of marketing strategies
- involvement in new stores and refurbishments
- establishment of quality management functions.

You can see that adding the major achievements gives a much more favourable impression of the applicant.

So what constitutes an achievement? Here is our list of criteria for job-related achievements:

- completing something successfully
- an outcome that can be attributed at least in part to you
- something that is measurable (profits, turnover, savings, words per minute)
- something that you can prove to have happened or that can be verified
- making a change or a difference.

Examples of achievements are:

- winning a customer-service award
- improving profits
- introducing a profitable product
- increasing the number of cars serviced per week
- reducing the number of customer complaints
- reducing the turnaround time for orders
- increasing the reliability of a service.

You have now re-written your CV using more positive language, emphasising all your achievements, so it is time to see if what you have passes the CV fitness test!

Remember from Chapter 2 how employers think about fit in terms of knowledge, skills, abilities and attitudes? Have you worked out:

- what experience is required for the job?
- the skills needed to do the job?
- the abilities that will be required?
- the sort of person/attitudes the employer expects?

Regarding you, have you included in your CV:

- relevant knowledge?
- relevant skills?
- demonstrated compatible abilities?
- demonstrated compatible attitudes?

If the CV passes the fitness test, you should now apply our Gestalt test! The next set of rules is not ours but comes from respected Gestalt psychology. These well-established rules were used to describe visual perception, but they apply equally well to CVs.

The Gestalt rules of CVs

1 Similarity: people will group together, as roughly the same, similar jobs and experiences.

2 Grouping: people will assume that things that are close together belong together. In other words, if you, say, were in a team that had a success, it puts you close to a success and the success will be associated with you.

3   Closure: people look for closure on projects and activities – can you demonstrate that you finished projects you started?

4   Continuity: people will assume that things that follow on closely in a similar pattern are part of a longer-term logical development.

Similarity

This can be used effectively on your CV. By emphasising the similarity of your previous jobs to the one you are applying for, you increase the fit between you and the job. Equally, similarity may govern what jobs to include and what to leave out of a CV. If you have a long work history, it may be sensible to concentrate on listing only those jobs that you have done in the past five to ten years, especially if these are the most similar to the one you are going for.

Here is an example of the similarity effect:

Employment history

1983–84	Receptionist, Blue Blot Ink Co.
1984–86	Secretary, Blue Blot Ink Co.
1986–92	Sales Assistant, Jeans R Us
1992 –93	Secretary, Hercules Music Company
1993 –99	Call Centre Operator, Big Brick Phone Co.
1999 –2000	Personal Assistant to CEO, Big Brick Phone Co.
2000 – Present	Personal Assistant to CEO, Slender Phones Pty

What skills would you describe this person as having? Most people would get the impression from this history that the candidate was a secretary. This is because the terms 'receptionist', 'secretary' and 'personal assistant' all conjure up ideas of similar jobs, whereas 'sales assistant' and 'call centre operator' seem dissimilar. The power of this effect can be seen when you add up the number of years doing the various jobs. This person spent more time (13 years out of 18) not being a secretary!

Closure

Closure is something that many employers will be looking for. They want to see that you can see things through, that you don't quit when the going gets tough.

Can you give examples where you completed a project successfully at work? Closure can also be demonstrated by showing that you moved to the next job because your work was completed in the old job, or that you had gained all the personal development likely: 'I moved on because I needed a new challenge having mastered my old job.'

Grouping

This is a powerful effect. If you were 'close' to some outcome, you will be associated with it. It is a bit like being at the scene of the crime – you automatically become one of the witnesses (and sometimes a suspect). Consider the following two work histories.

Negative grouping

I started in the commodities team, and moved on to sales when the team was disbanded. The sales were outsourced in 1995, when I joined the merchant division.

Positive grouping

I was part of the commodities team that broke all the market records, and then moved to sales, where the group achieved a 25 per cent improvement. This led to my current position in the merchant division.

You can see the power of grouping well here. The first example gives the impression of a loser and the second of a winner, despite the lack of evidence to suggest the candidate was responsible either for any of the successes or the failures.

Continuity

This relates most obviously to gaps in career history. We will spend some more time considering this later. However, it is worth pointing out here that most employers want to see continuity in employment. Continuity has two aspects. Firstly, have you been continuously employed over the years and, secondly, does your work history combine to tell a logical story or does it appear random? The following examples illustrate this point:

Continuous employment, but discontinuous types of job

1983–84	Receptionist, Blue Blot Ink Co.
1984–86	Assistant Chemist, Blue Blot Ink Co.
1986–92	Sales Assistant, Jeans R Us
1992–93	Product Packer, Hercules Music Company
1993–99	Stores Administrator, Big Brick Phone Co.
1999–2000	Sales Representative, Big Brick Phone Co.
2000–Present	Glazier, Heritage Doors Ltd

Continuous employment, and reasonably continuous types of job

1983–84	Receptionist, Blue Blot Ink Co.
1984–86	Secretary, Blue Blot Ink Co.
1986–92	Sales Assistant, Jeans R Us
1992–93	Secretary, Hercules Music Company
1993–99	Call Centre Operator, Big Brick Phone Co.
1999–2000	Personal Assistant to CEO, Big Brick Phone Co.
2000–Present	Personal Assistant to CEO, Slender Phones Ltd

From these examples, it can be seen clearly that the story of the first candidate's working life is a very confused and mixed one. It doesn't create a great impression. The second candidate's history tells a story of steady advancement (and therefore achievement) in the secretarial area. It is a much more positive story.

Now you know all about the Gestalt laws, use them to guide what goes into your CV and what does not, how to word your job history and how to present your CV. Once your CV passes the fitness test and the Gestalt test, you are ready to put the icing on the cake! In the next chapter, we discuss some techniques that we have demonstrated in our research to be effective.

9 Presenting your CV

In this chapter, you will learn how to:

■ set out your CV for maximum effect

■ use bullet points or continuous prose where appropriate.

We have already touched on some basic points about the best way to present your CV – we've seen that recruiters prefer simple typefaces and plain white paper. In this chapter, we look at successful presentation in more detail.

Layout

The first thing to say about the layout of your CV is do not put the words 'Résumé' or 'Curriculum Vitae' on the top of your CV. Quite apart from insulting the reader – what else could the document be? – it is a waste of valuable space.

At the top of the first page of your CV, put your full name (or the name you wish to be known by). It should be in bold type, at a size of 20 points, centred on the page. Leave plenty of white space below this heading, before you list your personal contact details.

Aligned on the left side of your page, give your address. Use the right-hand side on the same lines to give your telephone and fax numbers.

The remainder of your CV appears in the following order:

■ education details should come next (though there are variations on this)

■ professional associations

■ work history

■ references (if you include them) come last.

Headings

Headings have to be consistent in appearance. They must all be the same font and size. In the example given on page 105, there are three different levels of headings. The applicant's name is given in Arial, 20 points in size, and is in bold. The major sections 'Education' and 'Work history' are 14 points in size, in bold. Subheadings under 'Work history' are in 12 point, and the text is 10 point.

Making the same type of headings look the same is another example of the Gestalt law of similarity. The reader finds it easy to see the separate sections.

White space and grouping

You must leave plenty of white space on your CV. If you put too much writing on a page, your CV will be hard to read and look cluttered. You should also allow a generous margin of at least 2.5 centimetres on all sides.

White space can be used to apply the Gestalt principle of grouping (that things close to each other belong together). In the example, there is plenty of space between the person's contact details and their education. There are smaller gaps between their school and university, and then there is a larger gap again between education and the work history. The size of the gaps tells the reader that the things close together are all related. The larger gap indicates to the reader they are moving on to some different type of information.

Font

Use the same font throughout. Here are some good and bad examples:

The fast cat jumped over the lazy dog. (Arial)

The fast cat jumped over the lazy dog. (Times New Roman)

The fast cat jumped over the lazy dog. (Courier)

The fast cat jumped over the lazy dog. (Bookman)

The fast cat jumped over the lazy dog. (Comic Sans MS)

The fast cat jumped over the lazy dog. (Brush Script)

The fast cat jumped over the lazy dog. (Tekton)

The first two are both acceptable fonts; the second two are less acceptable, but still ok; the last three are definitely not suitable.

Bullet points or continuous prose?

We did some research to see if recruiters had a preference for work histories presented as bullet points or as continuous prose (that is, as a series of normal sentences). The results were not straightforward. Recruiters tended to prefer candidates to write complete sentences, but if the CV had been re-written by a recruitment agency, they tended to prefer bullet points!

So what should you do?

Bullet points are quick and easy to read, and look attractive on the page, as long as there are not too many of them. The risk with bullet points is that people tend to be too brief and the bullet point becomes meaningless. For example:

I have good working knowledge of Word and Excel and some experience of Lotus.

Compare this with:

- *Word, Excel, Lotus.*

The first sentence provides more information than the bullet.

If you are going to use bullet points, make sure that they are meaningful.

Finally it is worth noting that writing complete sentences allows you to show off your communication skills if your spelling and grammar are good.

Other important layout and presentation issues

Here are some other points to keep in mind:

- You should not use underline headings as it tends to look messy, and headings may also be misread by computer scanners. (More about this in Part 4.)

- Do not use both sides of the paper. People may forget to photocopy or scan both sides.

- You must have your CV laser-printed. Using old or cheaper printers is not acceptable now that high-quality laser printers are commonly available.

- Do not use colour in your CV. It often looks tacky and cannot be photo-copied easily.

- Do not put clip-art, cartoons or other illustrations on your CV. (Remember our advice about wacky CVs?)

- Use high-quality paper that is white (other colours may not scan or copy well).

- If you are sending out photocopies, ensure that the quality of the copy is excellent (a good copy is almost indistinguishable from an original).

- Do not fold your CV – buy an A4 envelope.

The following is an example of a well set-out CV, followed by the same CV set out poorly.

CV Example 1

IAN GREGORY CHAPPELL

360 Edgecliff Avenue

Wakefield

West Yorkshire

WF4 2NO

Telephone: 01924 523124 (home)

01924 523421 (work)

07803 644644 (mobile)

Fax: 01924 523422 (work)

Email: igchappell@hotmail.com

Education

1979 – 1985	St Mark of the Blessed Taylor High School, Leeds
1985 – 1989	Electrical Engineering, Salford University
	First Class Honours

Work history

1989 – 1994   Optus   Leeds

An international telecommunications company.

Communications Engineer

I was responsible…

Senior Communications Manager

I did…

1994 – Present   Telstra   Wakefield

Operations Manager

I am currently responsible for…

CV Example 2

Confidential CV of:

Name: Ian Gregory Chappell

Address: 360 Edgecliff Avenue, Wakefield, West Yorkshire, WF4 2NO

Telephone: 01924 523124

01924 523421 (work)

07803 644644 (mobile)

Fax: 01924 523422 (work)

email: igchappell@hotmail.com

Education

1979 – 1985

St Mark of the Blessed Taylor High School, Leeds

1985 – 1989

Electrical Engineering, Salford University, First Class Honours

Work History

1989 – 1994   Optus   Leeds

An international telecommunications company

Communications Engineer

I was responsible…

Senior Communications Manager

I did…

1994 – Present   Telstra   Wakefield

Operations Manager

I am currently responsible for…

Using white space

Which of the following CV layouts looks the best?

CV 1

CV 2

CV 3

CV 4

CV 5

CV 6

We think the outstanding winner is CV 2. The layout achieves a nice balance between the amount of information provided and the overall neat and tidy easy-to-read appearance. Secondly, this CV has used the Gestalt proximity rule (things that are close together will be assumed to belong together). In CV 2, although you cannot read the writing, you can clearly see the different sections. This makes the CV look more logical and structured – and we cannot even read what it is saying! Notice how this CV leaves larger margins at the top and bottom and on the left and right.

CV 3 is not too bad, although the structure is a little less clear. Ideally the CV should have definite sections – name, contact details, training/education, job history/skills. On this CV, it looks as though the name and contact details are all bunched together.

CV 1 is not too bad, but notice how the eye is drawn to the empty white space at the top right. It looks as though a photograph or picture has been removed. This layout might be a good idea if you are submitting an electronic CV or if you think that the CV is likely to be scanned into a computer. The alignment of the text on the left, and the fact that each new section starts at the left-hand margin, makes it less likely that a computer will mis-read your CV.

CV 5 is an example of people taking the idea of 'white space' a bit too far. Here the CV looks to contain very little information, and it suggests either that the candidate has little to offer, or that we are in for about ten pages of artistic minimalism!

CVs 4 and 6 are shockers! CV 4 is an example of what happens when the writer has not thought through what they want to say and therefore attempts to cram in as much as possible. Remember, less can often be more with CVs. The look of this CV is off-putting and suggests to the reader that they might need a couple of stiff drinks to help them get all the way through it. This layout can only be justified when the CV is being used for a proposal where a very strict page limit on the overall application is demanded, or perhaps where a candidate has been specifically asked (perhaps after interview) to provide a much more detailed background document. For the rest of you, if your CV resembles CV 4, re-write it immediately!

CV 6 is a mess. The boxes around the text are distracting and although they clearly indicate the various sections, the same effect can be achieved in a less heavy-handed manner with judicious use of white space (as in CV 2). Furthermore, these boxes may stuff up a computer scan of the CV. Resist the temptation to show off your skills with the Draw or Insert Picture commands on your word processor.

part two

the icing
on the cake

So now you have a CV, beautifully set out and crammed with achievements. You've baked your cake! Next, we show you how to improve your CV even further, by putting the icing on the cake. In this section, we explore the techniques that have been shown by our research to be successful in impressing recruiters.

10 Mind your language!

In this chapter, you will learn:

■ that language matters on a CV

■ which words can enhance a CV

■ which words and phrases can detract from a CV.

We have spent a lot of time discussing just how important it is to emphasise your results and successes on your CV, but this should not be at the expense of making sure the language on your CV is absolutely spot on.

Word power

When you list your achievements, pay attention to how you write them because the words you choose can have a huge influence on recruiters. Recruiters will judge your CV on how well you communicate, so choosing the right words is very important.

Think back to the beginning when we were discussing the importance of selling yourself. The words listed overleaf are examples of good 'selling' words.

overcame	achieved	enlarged	developed	discovered
controlled	managed	delivered	reorganised	won
applied	defeated	eliminated	engineered	overhauled
presented	founded	instigated	created	directed
attracted	led	initiated	established	enjoyed
contributed	modified	specialised	expanded	repaired
improved	analysed	coordinated	trained	organised
guided	conducted	implemented	built	designed
persuaded	helped	proved	utilised	simplified
investigated	completed	compiled	demonstrated	accomplished
transformed	introduced	finalised	headed	constructed
supervised	illustrated	outlined	selected	monitored

Words that can boost the power even more include:

quickly	successfully	rapidly	carefully	decisively
competently	resourcefully	capably	efficiently	consistently
effectively	positively	cooperatively	selectively	creatively
assertively	energetically	enthusiastically	responsibly	flexibly

Words with negative connotations should be avoided if possible. They include:

avoided	failed	succumbed	relied	conflicted
tried	disciplined	attempted	abandoned	unsuccessfully
lost	dismissed	withdrew	relinquished	argued

Write positively. It's all about Attitude!

Clichés

There are some warnings here and the first is beware of clichés. Clichés are overworn phrases that become meaningless and irritating. For instance, 'Have a nice day', or 'In a packed programme tonight…', or 'our world exclusive', or 'Unaccustomed as I am to public speaking…'. Unfortunately, the world of work has a peculiar love of clichés, so it is difficult to know when you are 'over-egging the pudding' (to use a cliché).

Avoid putting clichés in your CV. At best they will be disregarded, at worst they will irritate.

Here a few examples that are still okay to use:

Total quality	Beware not to overuse this term (e.g. total added value, or total global communication) etc (or the word 'quality')
Added value	(Yuk! But some people appear to like it)
Global	
Downsizing	
Rightsizing	
Outsourcing	
Focus	As in 'customer focus' or 'team focus' (but not total focus)

Now, read through your list of achievements and look closely at each word you have used. Is there another word that might make you look more impressive? If so, replace the word with the more positive one.

Technical language

Many jobs in the legal, medical, scientific and computing areas have lots of jargon words associated with them. It is always very difficult to know when and where to use such words. You can be sure it is safe to use words or phrases that appear in the job advertisement or description. If the employer uses simplified words or phrases to describe some technical aspect of a job, then you should also stick to the simplified words. However in this case it is permissible to provide more technical examples to illustrate your point.

For instance, if the advertisement says 'high level statistical knowledge required' it is permissible to include a statement such as 'I have a very high level of statistical knowledge, including the use of Multiple regression, analysis of variance and structural equation modelling techniques'. The first part of the sentence uses the same language as the advertisement, and the second part goes into more detail. If you had included only the second part of the sentence, it is possible that the person reading the CV intitially may not have the technical knowledge to appreciate that 'Multiple regression, analysis of variance and structural equation modelling techniques' are high level statistical techniques, and so your CV may be rejected.

Remember there is a fundamental imbalance between the applicant and the employer at this stage. It is permissible for the employers to use jargon terms that send you to the library seeking clarification, but do not be tempted to throw your own different jargon back at them – employers do not want to visit the library!

Some useful texts that can assist you more fully in this regard include:

- *The Elements of Style* (Allyn & Bacon)
- *Longman Grammar of Spoken and Written English*
- *Fowler's Modern English Usage*
- *The Oxford Dictionary for Writers and Editors.*

11 Using competency statements

In this chapter, you will learn:

■ how to construct a competency statement

■ how to increase job 'fit' with these statements.

What is a competency statement?

Put simply, a competency statement briefly outlines the knowledge, skills, attitudes and abilities you possess.

Think back to Chapter 2 where we talked about 'fit'. We showed you how employers think about jobs in terms of the knowledge required to do the job, the skills required to do the job, the attitude that is required, and the abilities required.

A competency statement should address all these points, and should serve to increase the perception of fit between you and the job in the employer's mind.

Include competency statements and back up with examples.

Here are some example statements created to emphasise some quality that an employer is seeking:

Highly motivated: I have a proven track record of achievement, both within university and through extra-curricular activities. I have won numerous awards throughout my academic career, but have still managed to maintain a balance with social activities.

Sales market knowledge: I keep in touch with the market by reading sales journals and magazines, as well as visiting supermarkets and other points of sale. Last year, I completed a research project entitled 'What makes a supermarket tick: Best placement or best product?', which looked at the dynamics of product placement in stores and the impact on sales.

Organisational skills: As a person who is involved in many different activities, I have developed excellent organisation skills to ensure that I plan my time effectively. This enables me to achieve maximum output in minimum time, as well as handle a number of activities simultaneously.

Energetic: I am a person who is always on the go, as I am involved in a number of activities. These range from academic to work-related to sporting, particularly team sports. I am an outgoing person and enjoy being an active member of numerous clubs and associations.

Communication skills: My diverse range of experiences at university, work and in extracurricular activities has enabled me to acquire strong verbal and written communication skills. As an outgoing person, I have also had numerous opportunities to develop my interpersonal skills to a high level.

Responsible: As a person who has always been involved in a range of activities, I have developed a responsible and mature approach to any task that I undertake, or situation that I am presented with. I believe that these assets will stand me in good stead for any future positions that I undertake.

You can see from looking at all of the statements, that each one addresses one aspect of a job. The words in bold are the words that the candidate has realised are critical components of the job from analysing the job advertisement.

Here is the job advertisement with the keywords in bold:

GRADUATE SALES ANALYST
Transform your career!

Step up to an organisation that's **really on the move globally**, with consumer and pharmaceutical products that consistently set a new standard for excellence at the world-class level.

As a crucial member of our 'Household Products' sales team, you will be working with leading brands. Your exceptional analytical ability will enable you to analyse market data, and **working closely with Account Managers** help build our brands in the market place. **Carefully monitoring** sales of our products, and our competitors', will be of prime importance. You will be more than just a 'number cruncher' in this role – you will develop an intimate understanding of how the grocery trade operates: both from the retailer and manufacturer's perspective.

We're looking for a person who is **motivated, keen to stay in touch with the marketplace**, and who can ably provide tactical support in achieving specific objectives.

Requirements for the position are tertiary qualifications in business, marketing or a related discipline. You may have some sales or retail experience, and a strong desire to pursue a **sales** career. A track record of **achievement** is essential!

You can see from an analysis of the advertisement what sort of qualities they are looking for in the job:

- 'really on the move globally' means energetic
- 'working closely with Account Managers' means communication and organisation skills
- 'carefully monitoring' means responsible
- 'motivated' and 'achievement' mean… highly motivated
- 'keen to stay in touch with the marketplace' means sales market knowledge.

The competency statement for each quality is simply a short sentence or two saying why you have those qualities. You can see how these sorts of statements try to emphasise the fit between the candidate and job more directly than a mere job history.

Do they work?

We were not at all convinced that such statements would be effective, but were amazed to find that, when we included them on CVs, they boosted our candidate's chances by as much as 30 per cent. In one study, one candidate's CV that did not include these statements was not shortlisted by any of our professional recruiters. When we put competency statements on the CV, one in three recruiters said they would interview the candidate! For another candidate, when the statements were included on the CV every recruiter said they would interview the candidate, whereas only eight out of 10 said they would interview the candidate when the statements were missing.

We were so surprised by these results, we did another study to check if we had made a mistake. We got exactly the same results.

Always include as much quantifiable data as possible when listing achievements.

Where should you put them on a CV?

We have tried placing these statements at the end of the CV, before the 'referees' section, and we have placed them at the beginning after the applicant's name. We've put them on the second page, and we've put them in the covering letter, all with exactly the same results. It does not seem to matter where you put them, as long as they are there. We usually put them under a heading: 'Knowledge, skills and abilities'.

Why do they work?

There are probably several reasons they are so successful. Firstly, you are picking up on the attributes the employer thinks are important and addressing each of them – it's a bit like answering an interview question like 'Tell me, do you have any sales market knowledge?'. You are talking the employer's language.

Secondly, you are making it easier for the employer to see the fit between you and the job, because you have taken the trouble to point out all the things in common. It may also make it easier for a computer scanner to pick out any keywords.

Finally, the very fact you've put this extra section on your CV shows you have thought a bit more deeply about the job and how you would fit it well. It makes you stand out from all those candidates that just list their skills and qualifications as if to say 'take it or leave it'.

Are they a bit over the top?

Very probably yes, but it doesn't seem to matter. In fact we found that the more competency statements we included on a CV, the more likely it was that the candidate was shortlisted for interview!

I bet this 'trick' doesn't fool experienced recruiters!

Yes and no. While it is true that younger or inexperienced recruiters are the most likely to be influenced by these statements, we found that even older and very experienced recruiters tended to shortlist CVs containing these statements more often than standard CVs.

How do you write a competency statement?

Firstly revisit Chapter 4, which tells you how to analyse a job advertisement. Then follow these easy steps:

1 Pick out the key qualities that the employer is looking for from the job ad. Qualities listed in Chapter 4 such as 'dynamic', 'great communicator' and so forth are common.

2 Go back through the templates of you and your achievements that you made earlier. How can you demonstrate these desired qualities? Have a look at the example competency statements in this chapter for some ideas on how to do it.

3 Read through what you've written carefully. Can you justify what you are claiming? If not, omit the statement – it is not acceptable to lie. If you are found out (which is likely), you could be fired from the job you get. Does the statement look really weak or unexceptional? If it does, omit it or strengthen it by giving concrete examples. Examples of statements that are probably too weak include: 'I get on well with people' (strengthen by giving examples), 'I am a likeable person' (strengthen by giving examples).

If you're having trouble coming to grips with this idea, look at the samples at the end of our book. These outline the types of competency statements to use in more detail.

Include competency statements on your CV!

The more competency statements you put on your CV, the more chance you have of being shortlisted.

12 Using career objectives

In this chapter, you will learn:

■ what a career objective statement is

■ whether they work

■ how to write a career objective statement.

What is a career objective statement?

A recent trend has been to include a career objective at the beginning of your CV. The career objective is a succinct statement that describes what you want out of a job. It allows the reader to get a quick idea of your suitability for the job advertised, and it also serves to make you appear more motivated.

Career objectives can be as simple as stating what sort of job you are looking for. For instance someone in the medical world might write:

Employment in a hospital specialising in care of the elderly.

These sorts of statements have their uses in letting the reader know quickly whether you are a serious contender for the job. However if the person in the above example would also be happy caring for young children, they may be narrowing their opportunities unnecessarily. Such statements might also be seen by the reader as rather obvious. (After all, they have applied for the job!)

A good career statement might read:

Accounts manager in a growing organisation, where I can use my communication skills to deal with a variety of clients.

The statement is positive, it doesn't sound too desperate, in the way that a statement like 'To work for your organisation' does, and it is not too limited.

A bad career statement starts:

All I've ever wanted to be was…

The statement above is a real example, and gives the impression of very limited ambition and narrow focus.

It is sometimes better to see the career objective as an opportunity to market yourself as well as stating what you want to do. The example below shows how you can slip in some positive comments about your skill levels and motivation.

A position as training manager in a progressive multinational company where I can maximise the use of my communication and teaching skills and where I will be continually challenged and stretched.

Do they work?

A lot of people get terribly self-conscious about using these sorts of statements. However, in a study we did with recruiters, we found that CVs that included career objectives influenced recruiters to think the applicants were more suited to the job they had applied for. So, yes, they do work and you should consider including one on your CV.

Career objectives probably become less effective the more experienced you are. They are certainly a good idea for young applicants, graduates and people in the first five or so years of their working career. They may also be a good option for people looking at changing careers.

As the name implies, they should be statements about your desired career, so they are not really appropriate for temporary jobs such as student vacation jobs. 'To develop my skills in waiting on tables…' doesn't sound quite right.

13 Job application letters

In this chapter, you will learn:

■ how to write an effective job application letter

■ why tailoring your letter to the employer is important.

What is a cover letter for?

All CVs should be accompanied by a cover letter. The cover letter has several purposes:

■ it lets administrative staff know quickly what the correspondence is about

■ it is often the first thing an employer reads

■ it allows you to say why you are applying

■ it sets the tone for the CV.

Many authors seem to suggest you produce fairly standard CVs and put your efforts into tailoring the cover letter. We do not think this is the best approach, and it should be clear that we believe you should tailor the CV for each job. One very sound reason for this is that it is the CV which usually gets more attention, and generally it is the CV that is used as the basis of questions asked in employment interviews (not the covering letter).

Cover letters should be taken seriously. However, do not think that a 'one size fits all' approach to your CV can be compensated for by a cover letter.

Application letter rules

Here are the basic guidelines for writing a letter of application for a job:

- you must write a new one for each application
- the addressee must be correct – do not cut and paste letters
- the date must be correct
- they should never be more than one page long
- they should be as well laid out as your CV
- unless a handwritten response is specifically asked for, you should type your letters.

Do not state information in the cover letter which can be obtained from reading your CV.

Your letter should include the following information:

- your (typed) name, address and phone number (with area code)
- the name of the person to whom you are writing (get this from the job advertisement, or phone the company and ask who you should address the letter to)
- their job title
- their address
- the initial greeting (for example, 'Dear Ms Smith,' or 'Dear Sir,')
- the first sentence, which should state:
  - the job you are applying for
  - reference number
  - where you saw the post advertised
- a couple of sentences that are catchy statements such as those we developed as competency statements in Chapter 8. ('I have over five years' experience as a machinist with Bloggs and Bloggs, and have experience of a wide variety of pattern techniques.)
- a couple of sentences about why this employer/job is right for you
- a polite request for a reply
- your signature and your name typed below it.

The following example will give you a guide.

Sample cover letter

Jenny Halse
15 Castle Street
Guildford, Surrey
GU3 2PS
Tel: (01483) 2934532

20 July 2001

Robert Wayne
Fabrication Manager
Laughing Boy Dog Toys
2 Railway Cuttings
East Cheam, Surrey
CR7 2OT

Dear Mr Wayne

I wish to apply for the position of machinist (ref 301/99) that was advertised in the *Evening Standard* on Friday, 20 July 2001.

I have over five years experience as a Machinist with Weaveanduck and have experience of a wide variety of pattern techniques. My technical skills are second-to-none, and I have an excellent record as a reliable, productive employee.

I am looking for new challenges and the position of Machinist sounds the perfect opportunity. Your organisation has an enviable record in innovation in machining, and an excellent reputation as an employer, making the position even more attractive.

I enclose my CV for your inspection and look forward to hearing from you soon. I am available for interview at your convenience.

Yours sincerely

Jenny Halse

part three

the doctor is in –
your
problems solved

At this stage you have put together a strong CV, and you have given it a shine and extra polish, but still there are those nagging questions about particular aspects of the CV. We hope that this part of the book will answer those questions for you.

14 Tricky CV issues

In this chapter, you will learn more about:

■ dealing with potential prejudice on the part of recruiters

■ dealing with gaps in your employment history

■ electronic CVs

■ the steps in the recruitment process

■ including referees in your CV

■ including a photograph in your CV.

Dealing with prejudice

One of the most commonly asked questions about writing a CV is what to do about bias. This is a really difficult one to answer, and we are sure there is no one correct way to go about this. Rather, you need to reflect on your own values when deciding what to do.

The first thing to say is that there is a lot of it about. The second thing to say very quickly is that for some groups, things are getting a bit better.

Bias exists in all forms and includes, but is not limited to:

■ ethnicity

■ gender

■ sexuality

■ marital status

- age
- health
- weight
- height
- beauty
- perceived social class
- address
- clothes
- political beliefs
- education
- physical disability.

Study after study has shown that recruiters are biased either deliberately or unconsciously, and (guess what!) the most successful job candidates are young, white, attractive, middle-class, well-educated males, followed by their female counterparts.

A recent study we conducted showed that people shown CVs containing photographs of the candidates were more likely to be influenced by the candidate's looks if the candidate was female. For men and women, the less attractive candidates were less likely to be shortlisted.

Strategies for dealing with this are very complex and personal.

One approach is to conceal information that may prejudice your chances of getting shortlisted. To some, we know, this can be extremely insulting. They are justifiably proud of themselves and see concealment of facts as playing up to the bigots. This is perfectly understandable, and that is where personal choice comes in.

Health, physical characteristics, age and marital status are information about yourself we suggest you generally omit. These are irrelevant to most jobs.

If you do decide to conceal your gender, ethnicity or sexuality on your CV, be sure that you do so consistently. If you have a French-sounding surname such as Depardieu, and you have mentioned that you speak fluent French, you will be assumed to be at least of French descent.

If you conceal your gender by using initials rather than first names, stating that you attended Horsham Ladies College is a dead giveaway!

Hobbies on your CV can be a giveaway, too (especially if you're branch secretary of the British Communist Party).

It is a sad fact that CVs that conceal some of the above items are more likely to be shortlisted.

While we despise this bias, it is reality, and it is up to you how you deal with it.

If you really wish to include any of the above information and are worried about the impact it may have, it probably means you would not be happy working for the organisation in question in the first place.

It is also worth remembering that just because the person who reads your CV may be prejudiced, this doesn't mean the people you will work with or for are also prejudiced. People working for recruitment consultants, or people working in human resources departments, may not be anything like the people you'll be working with!

A final point to make here, is that generally the bigger the organisation, the more likely it is to have Equal Employment Opportunities/Affirmative Action policies and officers. In theory, this should reduce problems of bias.

Gaps in career history

This is a difficult one, and when we studied several other commercially available CV guides we found that a couple advised that you explain gaps, a couple suggested you conceal gaps and a couple gave no advice!

So, we studied the impact of gaps of one year by giving recruiters a series of CVs, some of which had gaps that were explained, some that had unexplained gaps and some without gaps. We found:

- gaps were noticed 50 per cent of the time by recruiters
- if the gap was noticed and was not explained, recruiters thought the applicant was less honest than the average
- if the gap was noticed and explained, recruiters thought the applicant was more honest than the average
- only one out of ten reasons for a gap ('full-time academic study') was seen as a positive by recruiters
- redundancy, both voluntary and involuntary, is still seen poorly by recruiters, despite what some commentators say
- if the word 'caring' (as in 'caring for an ill parent') appeared in the explanation of a gap, the recruiters assumed the candidate was female.

Our advice is to explain any gaps – provided you have a good enough story to tell. Remember, the CV is often used at the interview stage to ask candidates questions. If the recruiters do not spot the gap during shortlisting, it is likely they will spot it at the interview.

If you have had a gap in employment for a very negative reason, such as imprisonment, you may wish to conceal it. However, you must never tell untruths in a CV. Lying about any aspect of your life during recruitment can be grounds for dismissal if uncovered.

If you are compelled to have many unexplained gaps in your work history, then it is almost certain that you should use either the functional CV or the structured interview CV. Both of these formats concentrate on skills and abilities and not on dates and times. Think back to the CV seesaw in Chapter 6. These CVs emphasise the right-hand side of the seesaw.

Electronic CVs

The development in electronic communications has brought about many new possibilities. We can now advertise jobs on the Internet, apply for jobs on the Internet, submit our CVs to sites on the Internet, email our CVs directly to employers, and we can set up personal web pages on the Internet.

Recruiters can now electronically scan CVs, in order to do all the screening automatically. Yes, it is now possible that only a computer will read your CV!

Finally, many more people now have access to word processors – which brings its own problems.

Tips for CVs that will be scanned

All scanners work on the same principles. They are looking for key words or phrases that have been programmed into the computer.

The words that companies scan for are often nouns and proper nouns, for instance, 'Excel' or 'Word' or 'automatic payroll systems'.

If you think it likely that your CV will be scanned electronically, this may be the time to use jargon or specialist language – provided that it is meaningful to people in your own industry. For instance, you might use terms like:

- AI (artificial intelligence)
- HTML (a computer programming language)
- ROI (return on investment)
- WYSIWYG (what you see is what you get).

Use lots of nouns and proper nouns to increase the chances that scanners will pick up on them.

Format is also important for scanned CVs. Layout should be clear and easy for a scanner to read.

The use of headings can assist here – remember, where you might otherwise refrain from using a heading for fear of insulting your reader's intelligence, computers do not have feelings, so spell everything out for them!

Headings such as the following may be useful:

- Experience
- Education
- Qualifications
- Work history
- Positions held
- Affiliations
- References.

The computer programs used to read your CV are becoming increasingly sophisticated, and therefore it is a canny idea to use some keywords to describe your personal qualities here too. Look back at the typical qualities that companies look for and, of course, the ones you have deduced from your detective work.

Words that might be useful here are:

- leader or leadership
- communicator
- sociable
- dynamic
- energetic
- excellent
- outstanding
- skilled
- intelligent
- team player
- team-focused

- outgoing

- persuasive

- dependable

- reliable.

Unusual fonts are never a good idea, especially when the CV might be scanned. Use Times, Times New Roman, Optima, Arial, Palatino, or Courier. The font size should be in the normal letter range of 10 to 14 point. Although earlier we suggested that a 20-point font for your name looks good, err on the side of caution if you think the CV is going to be scanned and use a smaller font.

If you include telephone numbers, list each one on separate lines, as a scanner may read numbers on the same line as one number. This will cause difficulties for people who subsequently look you up on a computer database when they want to contact you.

Underlining can make scanning more difficult, and doesn't look appealing generally, so desist.

The layout also affects the number of characters per line. In general, you should ensure that you do not have more than 70 to 80 characters per line, or scanning programs may reproduce the CV with some lines wrapped around onto the next line, causing the formatting to be messed up.

Avoid using columns like a newspaper. Start each new piece of information on a new line, fully aligned to the left. Look back to Chapter 9, where we compared different layouts. The best layout for a machine-readable CV is CV 1.

Do not put lines, pictures or graphics on your CV, as these will confuse the scanner.

Finally if you are mailing your CV to the employer using conventional mail, try to avoid folding it up to put it in an envelope. Put the CV in an appropriately sized envelope, and preferably one that has a reinforced cardboard back, to help prevent creasing.

Emailing CVs

As an alternative to mailing your CV, some employers now are happy to receive them electronically via email. This can speed up the recruitment process and can save money too. If you are applying for a job that requires some IT knowledge, then sending your CV by email will demonstrate that you are familiar with this type of technology.

There are a few pointers to take into consideration.

As with scanned CVs, you should keep to a maximum of 70 to 80 characters per line. Any more and you risk losing the formatting.

You should send the CV as an attachment. Do not be tempted to copy and paste it into the body of the email – you will lose most of the formatting. Remember, even though you may have a fancy email program that allows you to include formatting and graphics in the message body, the majority of email programs around do not allow this, and all you will do is send an unintelligible mess to your prospective employer.

If you do decide to attach the CV as a file, you need to consider carefully what word processing program you are going to use to generate the CV and, just as importantly, what version of the program you are going to use. Many large-scale commercial companies hold back from buying the very latest version of a piece of software because of cost, and to ensure that the new version is bug free.

Often the job ad will specify which programs are acceptable and which are not. If there are no guidelines, phone the company and ask. If this is not possible, the safest bet is to send a PC compatible file (not a Mac file), using Microsoft Word, Version 6 for Windows 95. It is a slightly older version, which means most people should be able to read it. Another safe bet is to save and send the file as 'Text only', but you will lose all your formatting by doing this, and you have to ask whether you are losing more than you are gaining by sending your CV by email.

CVs sent electronically may not be as secure as those sent by conventional mail. If your application is very sensitive, this point needs considering. Many companies now routinely monitor their employees' email and Net usage, making this a less confidential medium. One solution is to get your own email account. Many companies are now offering these free of charge. Alternatively, you could visit one of the Internet cafés and booths that are springing up in shopping centres, airports and high streets around the world. They will often provide a suitable service and may be able to assist you if you are unsure how the email process works.

Email is an easy and quick way to send things off. Resist the temptation to compose your CV and mail it off immediately. Many of us have had that sinking feeling just after we have hit the send button that we have sent the wrong version, sent it to the wrong person, or have included a glaring error.

Always print off a copy of your CV and have someone else read it before mailing or emailing it.

Web page CVs

Another innovation is the web page as a CV. These fall into two categories: individuals who build a personal web page and bring it to the employer's attention; and companies that allow you to enter your details either into their standard CV pro forma or by cutting and pasting your file onto their site. The CV is then indexed and stored on their site, for future employers to search through.

Personal web pages demonstrate the remarkable things that people will reveal about themselves that they'd never dream of including in a professional document!

Employers are generally not interested in 'meeting the babies', 'looking at my boat', or 'sitting in my front room'. If you intend to set up your web page as a substitute CV, then you must apply the same levels of professionalism as you would to a conventional CV. The key difference with a web page CV is that you can include far more information, provided it is appropriately indexed and the site is easily navigable. However, the initial key pages of the site should convey all the critical information of a conventional CV. Use the extra potential of a web site for additional optional information in links that employers can choose to follow.

Web site CVs become public documents, which potentially can be accessed by anyone, including your current boss! Do you really want all your personal details laid out for everyone to see?

Some valuable further resources on web-based CVs and the like are offered in Chapter 15.

What are the steps in the recruitment process?

There are no hard and fast rules about how people recruit, but the steps described below are fairly typical, though some firms will do things in a different order and some organisations will skip certain sections.

CV screening

This is what this book is all about! In this stage, recruiters narrow down the number of applicants by reading their CVs.

Sometimes this screening may involve a brief telephone interview with the recruiter before you are asked to submit a CV (and sometimes this telephone screening occurs after the recruiter has read your CV – there are no hard and fast rules on these stages).

Psychological testing or assessment centres

You may be asked to attend an assessment session, which could last between one hour and five hours (you will be told in advance).

You will be asked to complete pencil and paper tests designed to test your intelligence, personality, or particular skills such as reading and numeracy.

Interview

The interview stage may consist of one face-to-face interview, or it could involve a whole series of interviews on one day with different people or over a period of time.

A face-to-face interview is the most common and involves you being asked a series of questions about you and your thoughts on the job.

Panel interviews have several people at once interviewing you. Do not be nervous – these are often fairer than the face-to-face variety.

The questions you get asked here might be prompted by your CV or the results of your psychological testing. Be prepared to explain any gaps on your CV, or to describe any aspect of your work history. It is here that liars are easily caught out.

Offer or rejection

About a week to four weeks after the deadline for applications closes, you are likely to hear whether you are being invited for an interview. Unfortunately employers are often slower to send out rejection letters.

You can expect to hear the outcome of an interview a bit more promptly. Often people have arrived home from the interview to find a voice mail message for them saying 'Congratulations!'

If you are offered the job, take your time to let things sink in before accepting. Most employers will give you a little time to think things over, but do not expect them to give you very long. Often there is a second good candidate who they do not wish to lose, should you turn them down.

If you are unlucky enough to be rejected, then join the club! You are in the overwhelming majority. Nearly everybody has been turned down for a job at some time or another.

Do not write an abusive letter or make an abusive phone call to the recruiter or employer – this is highly unprofessional and will risk your reputation with that employer and other prospective employers who get wind of your behaviour.

Sometimes, and we stress sometimes, some employers are willing to provide feedback to you if it is asked for in a polite positive manner, and the purpose is to assist you in strengthening future job applications. However many employers rightly fear that prolonging the dialogue may expose them to legal action or might mislead the candidate. Sometimes it really is luck of the draw.

Do I include referees and, if so, who should they be?

There is mixed advice from recruiters on this topic. Our preference is to include referee contact details as the last item on your CV. The reason for saying this rather than 'Referees available on request' is that it makes it easier for the employer. They do not have to make an extra call to get names and addresses. We also wonder how many people who have put 'Referees available on request' have panicked when asked for them because they hadn't bothered to work out who the referees would be!

Known to us personally are at least ten examples of candidates who have unwittingly continued to use a referee who has written extremely negative things about them. On other occasions, it is clear that the candidate has failed to ask the permission of a referee in advance when comments such as 'Last time I had contact with him he was unemployed in Cardiff' are made. This brings us to our next golden rule.

Always ensure that you know your referee well, and that they are happy to write or say something positive about you.

Not only should you ask the referee's permission, you should treat them with respect. That means you should inform them what sort of job you are applying for (you don't want a referee to express surprise on the phone). Do not abuse your referee by making them respond to hundreds of different employers that you have indiscriminately applied to.

The best referees are people who have supervised you in your recent jobs, especially the one you currently hold. Not only does this look more impressive, it tells the employer that you are not at loggerheads with your current supervisor. If this is not practical (because you are trying to maintain confidentiality), try using someone who has previously supervised you and has left the company or now works in a different area. Whatever you decide, remember that it is important to have as recent a referee as possible, since this is most likely to relate to the position you are applying for.

If you cannot get a reference from a current or recent employer, or alternatively, the job ad has asked for 'character references', you need to approach some other people. This is going to cause outrage among some readers, but there are some people who are more suitable than others. In general, people in 'professional' jobs are generally seen as 'good' referees:

■ lawyers

■ judges

■ teachers

■ lecturers

■ police officers

■ government councillors

■ company directors (but the company needs to be respectable)

■ senior managers.

Here are a few horror stories and perhaps some urban myths:

■ 'the best way of getting rid of a poor employee is to provide them with a brilliant reference'

■ candidates who invent their own references

■ candidates who use relatives with different names as referees.

We have genuinely seen a CV where the candidate had included a statement from a referee, who was his best friend's mother, and that was dated more than 14 years before! And another where a candidate using a false name and address of a referee turned out to be himself using a fake Scottish accent. Unfortunately for him, the accent wore off as the reference progressed and he said some unbelievably good things about himself. Needless to say, neither of these applicants got the job!

Do I include a photograph?

There are some things we strongly suggest you 'conceal', and this especially applies to photographs. Do not include one. Our reasons are:

1   We recently did a survey of a large recruitment firm's archive of CVs and could not find a single photograph attached to a successful CV.

2   In another more recent survey we carried out, of over 625 CVs sent to a recruitment firm, only seven included photographs. Interestingly, six of these candidates were male.

    There were twice as many males as females, but the males were six times more likely to include a photograph than females. Furthermore, not one of the candidates who attached a photograph was shortlisted, compared with 17 per cent of the candidates who did not include a photograph.

3   Not everyone looks like a supermodel, or photographs like one.

4   Sending a photograph is telling employers: 'I want to be judged on my looks and not on job-relevant characteristics'.

5   In a study completed as this book went to press, we compared identical CVs that included a photograph of a person who was independently judged to be attractive or unattractive. The results were depressingly inevitable: attractive candidates were judged more suitable for the job and were more likely to be shortlisted compared with unattractive candidates. This goes for men as well as women.

    Interestingly this beauty bias was more evident for women applying for a clerical position than for women applying for a higher-status legal position. We also found that it did not matter whether the job involved seeing clients or customers – attractive candidates were still more highly rated.

What are recruiters thinking when they read CVs?

We have extensively researched this question and it is clear that certain themes emerge. Below we provide a list of comments that have been collected in a series of systematic CV experiments. The comments all come from professional recruitment personnel and human resources officers.

Read through these statements – we believe they give you a unique insight into how recruiters think about the CV screening process. Notice how the comments vary from recruiter to recruiter.

Notice also that much of what they are saying is reflected in the advice we have given you in this book. Our advice comes from studies conducted with these professionals and augmented with our professional experience.

All the statements in this section are direct quotes taken from interviews and surveys with professional recruiters. The comments refer to CVs we asked the recruiters to read and screen as if they were taking part in a typical recruitment exercise. We asked recruiters which CVs they liked and why, the problems with the CVs they did not like, and how they came to make their decisions.

What do recruiters like most in CVs?

The three factors they appreciated most were:

1 Relevant experience.

2 Layout.

3 Qualifications.

Here are five examples of recruiters' comments about CVs they rated highly because of relevant experience:

1 Clear employment history, attributes clearly organised. CV very well put together and quite clear.

2 Clear direct description of experience in relation to the competencies described.

3 Computer skills, people skills, experience dealing with managers. A team player, thorough, ambitious.

4 Relevant work experience. Excellent mathematical skills. Strong track record of experience.

5 Scope of experience, ability to work and coordinate job role unsupervised.

Now see why layout is important in these comments from our team of recruiters:

■ Good, clear layout, highlighted awards.

■ Clear, well-ordered, logical, easy to read. Stable and relevant employment since March 94. Excellent academic qualifications.

- Responds to specific needs in the ad. Very well presented, clearly described details of experience and outcomes.

- Bold headings, logical layouts (qualifications should be on page one). Tasks, duties, position all very clear.

- Highlights those experiences most relevant to the job. Phrasing and format gave strong impression of qualities relevant to the position.

The recruiters responded to CVs emphasising qualifications in this way:

- Tertiary qualifications. Work experience relates to job requirements. Business information skills. Relevant extracurricular activities. High level of analysis and motivation. Layout of CV.

- Major assignments and rewards. Length of time employed and duties successfully undertaken while employed. Initiative in having own business.

- Degree project work (results on paper). Education. Work history. Marketing knowledge.

- Relevant work experience, mix of administration, customer service, analysis. Relevant study/qualifications exposed to systems. Easy to read, well laid out.

- Combination of qualifications, communication skills, expansion on experience, evidence of drive, energy, appropriate focus and experience.

What do recruiters dislike in a CV?

Here are five examples of comments made by recruiters about CVs they did not like, starting with relevant experience:

1 Very little experience (in time spent), too theoretical, that is, skills are demonstrated in education, not in work force. University results (although comprehensive) show weaknesses in areas of most importance.

2 Previous employment history does not exactly mix with the role being applied for.

3 Academic, little experience. Lacks ambition and enthusiasm, no continuity of employment.

4 Not as much relevant experience although shows initiative through own business. Layout of CV a little difficult to read.

5   Mainly research experience. Concerns about how applicant would go in the real world.

Poor layout can leave a poor impression on recruiters, as these examples show:

- Layout of CV terrible. Information too difficult to make sense of.

- Format annoying. Information irrelevant to this job.

- CV all over the place. No logic, difficult to follow. Can't be bothered persevering to find information.

- Little reference to position description. Poor point size. Bad layout with two columns. Very busy CV.

- Too much information per page. No logical sequence. Text is very small, though information is very good.

Recruiters looking for qualifications react very negatively when they're not there. For example:

- No demonstration or examples of the required/desired competencies. Nothing outstanding that would lead to thinking there may be special qualities.

- Does not show academic results. Poor detail on positions held.

- Job advertisement is looking for someone with a strong desire to pursue a sales career. This applicant has been 'back room'.

- Limited experience while working in buying field. Comparing CVs, this one has the least experience (in uni and work).

- Leaves me with the feeling that I need to be informed of more detail to appropriately gauge the candidate's suitability.

How do recruiters use job competencies to discern a good 'fit'?

In a recent study we looked at the effectiveness of including competency statements on CVs. Taking a sales analyst's position as an example, we asked a team of professional recruiters to list, in order of importance, the ten competencies they most valued and comment on them. We then counted the number of times all the recruiters mentioned those competencies in their comments.

The result in the following table reflects that count, showing the competencies the recruiters regarded as important for the position of sales analyst. (If we carried out this exercise for a different position, for example a laboratory technician, the results would be very different.)

Competency	Number of times mentioned
Communication skills	31
Numerical skills	26
Planning and organising	20
Market knowledge	19
Achievement orientation	17
Initiative with responsibility	16
Problem solving	11
Motivation	11
Energy	6
Tenacity	3

As you can see, an overall pattern emerges suggesting that communication skills and numerical skills were regarded as the most important. This supports the idea that recruiters build up their own opinions of which competencies are ideal for a particular position, in this case a sales analyst.

Here are some samples of why the different recruiters thought the different competencies were important for the sales analyst position.

Most valued competencies	Recruiters' comments
Achievement orientation	This is needed to keep up the level of motivation and move from an analysis role to a sales-oriented role in the future.
	Applicant needs to be an achiever with an understanding of the business, driven to assist Account Managers.

Most valued competencies	Recruiters' comments
Achievement orientation with communications skills	Any sales role needs a track record of demonstrable success. Communication skills are critical in sales.
Achievement orientation with initiative and responsibility	The applicant needs drive, ability and tenacity to meet goals. A graduate should be questioned about the responsibility to undertake activities and see them through.
Achievement orientation with numerical skills	This new position depends on achieving results in increased sales/market share. Key technical skill is the ability to collect and process relevant data. If this was not applicable, then communication skills would be ranked highest. This sales analyst role is to provide crucial information to assist in final sales. It requires extensive analysis.
Achievement orientation with planning and organising skills	The successful candidate must be goal oriented to handle this position which will need planning and organising skills because it is a new role.
Communication skills	This is the most valued competency because you can achieve anything with good communicators. There is internal and external liaison involved. Analysts need to get their conclusion across to their managers as well as clients. Customers demand excellent communication skills and a commitment to deliver.
Communication skills with initiative and responsibility	Written, oral and listening skills form the key to succeeding in this role. The role needs a person who will work diligently without constant supervision.
Communication skills with market knowledge	This role requires collective market/product information and collating in a form that can be used by clients. Experience in a team environment is required to deal with many parties, and to distribute information. It's clearly important for the applicant to have some idea of, and background in, the market area involved.
Communication with problem-solving skills	The concerns of customers will always need a high level of problem-solving.

Most valued competencies	Recruiters' comments
Communication with numerical skills	Ability to communicate with a wide range of people, know how the industry operates and interpret requirements for analysis is imperative.
Communication with planning and organising skills	Verbal ability to liaise with customers/peers/managers essential. Excellent written communication required in user-friendly presentation of data/results. Applicant will need to be a self-starter who is able to plan and organise own schedule.
Energy	Customer and account manager service will be directly affected by the energy and 'urgency' of the person who fills this role.
Initiative with responsibility	The role needs a person who takes their workload seriously and responsibly and creates efficiency through reduced human resource management. The applicant must be able to take on responsibility, empower people, and be able to take knocks and bounce back.
Initiative with responsibility and achievement orientation	Initiative and responsibility need to be established as priorities otherwise all else is affected. Respect, awareness and commitment are paramount, particularly within a team environment.
Initiative with responsibility and problem-solving skills	As the role reports to several managers, the applicant needs to be a self-starter. The role is analytically focused with the need to collect data and work through it piece by piece, as well as see the big picture, to get results.
Initiative with responsibility and tenacity	This person needs less direction, and will produce a higher work output of greater quality than others.
Market knowledge	The ability to monitor products from their own and a competitive situation is essential to the business performance. Important to understand what the products are, and where they sit in the market place.
Market knowledge with communication skills	Proof of efforts to understand and research market areas is essential. Manner is as important as ability and aptitude.

Most valued competencies	Recruiters' comments
Market knowledge with planning and organising	The role requires a good understanding of the market to perform the job to the best ability.
Motivation	Enthusiasm will allow even the least competent to shine.
Motivation with energy	These competencies are by far the most important. Without them, you will only ever be employed as an assistant sales analyst. These competencies are far in excess of the need for the candidate to be a graduate.
Motivation with initiative and responsibility	To provide constant and accurate reports to both customers and colleagues.
Numerical skills	You can't analyse if you can't do the sums. The role involves evaluation of sales forecasts versus actuals. Without good numerical analysis skills in this area, the business could lose sales.
Numerical skills with communication	The role requires numerical reasoning and understanding. Liaison with account managers, market place providers and users has to be clear and concise. This role includes analysis of data, sales forecasts and monitoring of pricing, as well as liaison, report preparation and promotion strategies.
Planning and organising	The applicant needs good skills in this area to cope with the volume and variety of work, and juggle the number of people to report to.
Planning and organising with communication skills	Given the number of projects involved in this role and account manager liaison, the ability to plan and organise oneself is critical. The need to liaise with customers, gather information and determine their needs makes communication skills critical.
Planning and organising with numerical skills	The role involves organising and planning data collection and collation. Statistical skills in analysing results is essential. There are many reports and analytical work required on sales and marketing issues.

Most valued competencies	Recruiters' comments
Planning and organising with problem-solving skills	This competency requires an ability to collate and deliver information to others, a need to ascertain and analyse data and evaluate various information
Problem-solving	Good problem-solving skills are necessary to support the numerical skills in evaluating and reporting market information. The role requires exceptional analytical ability.
Tenacity	People with tenacity are more likely to succeed than people who rely on any other individual competency.

As a contrast to the information given on the previous pages, we asked recruiters to list which of ten different competencies was their least valued when recruiting somebody into the position of a sales analyst. And again, we counted the number of times they mentioned those competencies.

Competency	Number of times mentioned
Tenacity	34
Energy	33
Motivation	18
Market knowledge	9
Numerical skills	9
Problem-solving	7
Initiative with responsibility	5
Achievement orientation	3
Communication skills	3
Planning and organising	1

Tenacity and energy were the least-valued competencies, followed by motivation. As was the case with the most-valued competencies, there is a strong opinion among the recruiters about the competencies that are not so important when preparing a CV for the sales analyst position.

Here are samples of the recruiters' comments about why they considered the various competencies were of little value.

Most valued competencies	Recruiters' comments
Achievement orientation	It is a backroom role and tends to be fairly process-oriented. Someone with a strong achievement orientation could become bored.
	This job does not require someone dominant in nature, as long as the job gets done within the time frame.
Communication skills	Person needs only to communicate internally at this stage with no client contact.
Energy	Energy is good but knowledge and efficiency is more important.
Initiative with responsibility	The applicants do not need as much of this because the position is a junior role.
Market knowledge	This can be learned within months on the job.
	This is a graduate position and market knowledge would not be envisaged at this point.
Motivation	It is hard to tell this competency from CVs. It's needed but is not as important if goals are achieved.
	This person may be in the role for some time before promotion.
Numerical skills	All candidates should have this skill but other competencies rank more highly because part of the position relates to personal and other skills.
Planning and organising	The person will report to line managers so their responsibilities will be structured.
Problem-solving	As the role is predominantly about producing reports from available data, this is not so important.
	The person would be under the wing of the sales manager and could develop this skill over time
Tenacity	The position has been created to support the sales team. The candidates should not have to sell their services. Tenacity is useless when gathering information.

What do recruiters think about when they make decisions on CVs?

We asked two recruiters to think out loud when reading CVs. We recorded their thoughts on each, then grouped them according to the recruiter's shortlisting decision.

Recruiter 1

Shortlist decision	Recruiter's comments
CV rejected	• The CV includes mistaken terminology for 'customers'.
	• It is reasonably articulate but the applicant's grammar and communication skills are questionable.
	• The letter is too long. It taps into a few things about the role advertised, but focuses on marketing, not sales.
	• The applicant has an associate diploma instead of the necessary degree.
	• The applicant describes skills but the ad says the employer wants a demonstrated track record of achievement.
Unsure of CV at this stage	• It's too short and includes the applicant's marital status which is irrelevant and annoying.
	• I question their expectations, but I like the covering letter.
	• I'm not into what they think they're good at. I'd prefer to see what they have done.
	• I need to know how much business experience the applicant has had.
Interview granted, based on CV	• The candidate is able to demonstrate achievement
	• The candidate worked all the way through university.
	• The CV demonstrates the candidate can manage a number of tasks.

Shortlist decision	Recruiter's comments
	• The candidate lists financial forecasting, statistics, computer literacy. • It was an average CV, but the candidate has a good academic record.

Recruiter 2

Shortlist decision	Recruiter's comments
CV rejected	• The CV is very hard to read. • There is too much school education. The university section is better laid out. • The only interesting thing in the CV is that the candidate 'speaks Japanese'. • There is nothing to support the candidate's original claims. • The candidate includes too much detail about extracurricular activities.
Unsure of CV at this stage	• The letter is quite interesting. The candidate starts off by saying what they do now and how they might relate to this job. • The candidate has retail experience, but the position doesn't need this. • Computer skills are important and the CV is well laid out. • The format of the CV is easy to scan.
Interview granted, based on CV	• In terms of key criteria, the competencies listed on the CV include achievement orientation and cooperation. • The interesting format makes me interested in the candidate. • Putting the candidate's attributes up front is a good idea.

How do recruiters decide between CVs in shortlisting?

We asked recruiters to list the most common strategies they used in short-listing. Here are some of their answers.

Recruiters' strategies for shortlisting CVs

1 The quality of written words and the structure of the cover letter.
2 Relevant experience.
3 Evidence of activities that indicate the nature of the applicant.

1 Academic qualifications are reviewed first, followed by a scan of the cv.
2 The structure of the covering letter is very important. Spelling mistakes are frowned upon.
3 Attention is focused on recent work experience.

1 Look for experience that approximates what is required.

1 Match candidate's competencies with the position.
2 Match work experience with the position.
3 Check the candidate's tertiary qualifications.

1 Compare the candidate's experience and qualifications with their competencies.

1 Read the CV thoroughly.
2 Review the competencies.
3 Consider how the CV matches the competencies.
4 Re-evaluate the CV.
5 Make a decision on whether to reject it or recommend an interview.

1 The candidate's knowledge, experience and personal traits are compared with those required for the position.

1 Read the cover letter to evaluate the standard of writing and the ability to address advertisement requests.
2 Then scan CV to check education and experience requirements are met before reading the CV in depth to gauge the candidate's level of achievement, responsibility, team involvement, etc.

1 Qualifications, experience.
2 Evidence of literacy, expression, numeracy.
3 Potential, apparent focus.

Do recruiters eliminate CVs on one piece of information?

Again, here are a few sample responses from our recruiters.

Eliminating CVs on one piece of information
Yes. I eliminated one candidate because they had a poor covering letter and errors in the CV. This indicates lack of attention to detail and care.
Yes, because of spelling errors and poor grammar.
I look to include applicants rather than to eliminate them, but I finally rank and select the strongest candidates.
No, never.
I am definitely put off by typos, spelling and grammar errors. If you can't get it right when you're trying to make a good impression, what about every day?
Not really, it is a matter of one CV not being as good as another CV.
I look for the amount of information around achievements.
If a degree does not include a relevant major, I query real interest in the job and ability to perform. This, combined with very limited experience in the area, means they would not be considered for interview.
No. At least a couple of factors worked together.

Our professional recruiters tell you their one best tip

Each recruiter was asked to nominate a single piece of advice for writers of CVs. Here are their comments:

- Make sure you have correct grammar with no spelling errors in the covering letter and address the competencies required in the advertisement.

- The CV should contain a clear concise and chronological format.

- Highlight the skills that meet the criteria and market and write with a positive attitude.

- Remember that you are marketing yourself, so while the integrity of the document is a must, the CV needs to present your best qualities and must detail your relevant skills and competencies.

- Include specifics like 'I achieved a 30 per cent increase in sales through the telesales initiative I introduced'.

- Do not overstate facts in the cover letter that can be obtained from reading the CV.

- Keep your CV short and to the point.

- Tailor the CV to suit the requirements of the ad and include achievements, not just duties, because these are what will sell you.

- Include examples to back up your competency statements.

- Follow my 4-S rule: Keep your CV Simple, Structured, Succinct and Significant.

- Make sure your CV supports the advertised position criteria and the feel of the ad without waffling.

- Use a sharp covering letter and restrict the CV to two pages. Identify your strengths and weaknesses, if possible. Emphasise aspects of your background which have an immediate or apparent match with the job requirements.

- Put your major achievements and accomplishments in the CV, not just tasks and responsibilities.

- Avoid being repetitive in your CV.

- Use active voice to describe what you have done in previous positions, and say why you want the job.

- Do your homework prior to applying. Find out about the company, obtain an annual report if available, find out what future projects the company might be involved with, who their clients are, who their competitors are.

- Clearly address the specific requirements called for so that the skills can be easily measured against the criteria, and then against those of the other applicants.

- Provide as much information as possible on work experience and tertiary education.

part four

resource bank –
ingredients & tips

In the last part of this book, we have provided you with some valuable resources to assist you in your CV preparation and job-seeking. Increasingly job-seeking and job applications are being conducted via the Internet, so we have provided you with some useful links. Given the nature of the Internet some of these inevitably will have changed in one way or another by the time you read this. However, we trust there will be enough useful sites to get your net-surfing started!

We have also included some sample CVs for you to look at in relation to the earlier chapters. We would emphasise, though, that we believe you should tailor your own CV to each specific job, so while we hope these CVs give you some ideas and inspiration, it is not our goal for you just to copy them. We hope if you have read the book up to this point, that you will have been persuaded by the scientific evidence and the feedback from recruiters that tailoring your own CV provides you with the best chance of producing a CV that gets short-listed. Good luck in your job-hunting.

15 Internet sites and other resources

The Internet is a great tool to search for jobs, post your CV, get some career tips and find out more about the companies you are interested in applying to. We debated about providing web addresses because of the high turnover of sites, so please accept our apologies in advance if any of the information has changed. Most useful are the sites held by the big search engines (see Altavista Careers or Excite Careers, for example). These have useful links to other related sites. To search the web for yourself, use terms like 'jobs' + 'UK'.

For some resources to help you in your job and advertisement research, check out the following sites.

Trade specific

www.siteworkjobs.co.uk	engineering, building trade
www.justengineers.net	engineering
www.jobsgopublic.com	public sector
www.thepeoplevillage.com	IT contractors
www.jobinga.com	games industry
www.ifi.co.uk/job.htm	environmental jobs
www.mtselect.co.uk	motor trade
www.education-jobs.co.uk	education

General sites

www.taps.com
www.jobserve.com
www.newmonday.com
www.gojobsite.co.uk

www.planetrecruit.co.uk
www.stepstone.co.uk
www.monster.co.uk
www.europa.eu.int
www.manpower.com
www.pricejam.com
www.jobsearch.co.uk
www.jobsunlimited.co.uk
www.topjobs.co.uk
www.jobsearch.org
www.jimbright.com   (*a CV writing service via the Internet*)

Government site

www.worktrain.gov.uk

A more detailed listing is provided below.

Site name	Web address	updates	post CV	career advice	post jobs	company info
America's Job Bank	www.jobsearch.org		✓		✓	
CareerBuilder	www.careerbuilder.com	✓		✓	✓	
Careermart	www.careermart.com		✓		✓	✓
Careermart Hi-tech	www.careermarthi-tech.com		✓		✓	✓
CareerPath	www.newcareerpath.com		✓		✓	✓
Careers Online	www.careersonline.com			✓		
Employment.com.au	www.careermosaic.jobs.com	✓	✓		✓	✓
Excite Careers	www.excite.co.uk/ jobs_and_careers/	✓	✓	✓	✓	✓
Fairfax General Employment	www.mycareer.com.au	✓	✓	✓	✓	✓
FastCompany	www.fastcompany.com		✓			
Headhunter.net	www.headhunter.com		✓	✓	✓	✓
Hot Jobs	www.hotjobs.com		✓		✓	✓
Jobnet	www.jobnet.com		✓		✓	✓

Site name	Web address	updates	post CV	career advice	post jobs	company info
Job options	www.joboptions.com	✓	✓		✓	✓
Jobs at Microsoft	www.Microsoft.com/jobs		✓		✓	✓
Jobs Unlimited	www.jobsunlimited.co.uk	✓	✓		✓	
JobSearch UK	www.jobsearch.co.uk		✓		✓	
Jobsite UK	www.jobsite.co.uk		✓	✓	✓	✓
Manpower	www.manpower.com		✓	✓	✓	
Monster	www.monster.co.uk	✓	✓	✓	✓	✓
Net-Temps	www.net-temps.com		✓		✓	
Oz search	www.ozsearch.com.au	✓	✓	✓	✓	✓
Price Jamieson	www.pricejam.com		✓		✓	
Recruiters Online	www.recruitersonline.com		✓		✓	
SEEK	www.seek.com.au		✓	✓	✓	✓
Top Jobs On The Net	www.topjobs.co.uk		✓	✓	✓	✓

This table was correct at the time of printing. Unfortunately, many web sites are not maintained and may be out of date. On the other hand, new web sites continue to appear.

Sample CVs

Here we offer you some examples of job advertisements and CVs applying for the positions.

School leaver sample

Adam Oakes

Address:	19 Boulevard Rd	Telephone: (020) 8670 5432
	Somerton Park, London SE24 4TP	Email: Oakes@btinternet.com

Career objective

I am looking for a busy, entry-level position in administration that utilises my computing and organisational skills while enabling me to learn about a business from the ground up.

Skills, experience and personal attributes

Communication skills

I have been developing my public speaking skills while competing in the Rostrum public speaking competitions. This experience has given me the confidence to express myself clearly and confidently. As a finalist in the Rostrum public speaking competition, I was invited to present to no less than 200 people. I regularly use my written communications skills in the composing of correspondence and promotional material for the Interact club.

Time management skills

While completing my A-levels I have held down a part-time position at Harvey Norman as well as being a Ranger Scout. These extracurricular activities have put additional demands on my time and without careful planning, my school work would have suffered. I have never missed a school deadline or needed an extension to complete work. To make the best use of my time I schedule it and complete tasks in order of priority. I believe these time management skills will transfer well to the workplace.

Customer relations skills

While at Harvey Norman, I have helped many customers, resulting in my being awarded 'Employee of the Month' four times. I take time to listen to customers, identify their needs and then recommend products that are most suitable. While at Harvey Norman I have attended a two-day training course on Customer Service Skills.

Computer skills

During my lower six year at High School, I completed a course in Computer Studies. This included Excel, Word for Windows, Access and Powerpoint. I was ranked second in my class for Computer Studies and feel that I am highly proficient in use of the packages. As a keen computer user at home, I am also familiar with Netscape and Eudora.

Education

Secondary

1998–2000	A-levels, South London High School
	Subjects: English; Economics; Computer Studies;
	General Studies

Other courses

1999	Customer Service Skills
	In-House Harvey Norman

Academic achievements

May 1999	Ranked top student in Economics at South London High School
Nov 1991	Rostrum Public Speaking Competition Finalist

Employment history

Feb 1997 – Dec 1999   Secretary, Interact Club, South London High School

Duties included:

- taking minutes of weekly meetings
- composing and typing outgoing correspondence
- organising mail-outs to students on club activities
- actioning in-coming correspondence
- typing up minutes from interact meetings.

Achievements:

- awarded with school prize for community involvement
- membership increased from 10 to 17 members following mail-outs that I initiated
- all in-coming mail dealt with within 7 days of receipt.

Feb 1998 – Dec 1999   Service Assistant (part-time), Harvey Norman, Croydon

Duties included:

- helping customers with location of products

- explaining different features of products to customers
- dealing with customer complaints when products returned
- serving customers at cash registers
- stocking shelves with products.

Achievements:

- 'Employee of the month' May 1998, Nov 1998, Feb 1999, July 1999, September 1999 (based on customer nomination)
- awarded employee with 'Best knowledge – bathroom fittings' by Caroma (supplier).

Interests and activities

Meeting new people, computing, public speaking

Referees

Mr John Norman, Store Manager, Harvey Norman: (020) 8272 4888

Ms Shirley Neavis, Team Leader, Harvey Norman: (020) 8272 4889

Graduate applicant

GRADUATE ENGINEER

ASM Power is setting a dynamic pace in the UK standby power market. Our current Operations and Engineering Managers joined as graduates, and their rapid progression creates openings for new graduates.

A structured two-year development programme will see you master a broad engineering/operations/management role. Commitment and enthusiasm will be required as you become involved in Production/Capacity Planning, Purchasing, Customer Liaison, Personnel Management, Process Re-Engineering and Supplier Negotiations.

You will need confident speaking and presentation skills, high computer literacy, and a willingness to embrace new ideas. Above all, you will recognise a great opportunity.

Send applications by June 5th to:
David Bradshaw, HR Director, ASM Power
New Industrial Estate, Croydon CO1 1MN

Kerry Hill

Address: 11 Ridgley St, Beckenham, Kent BR 6AB

Telephone: (020) 8234 5678

Mobile: 0701 329 897

Email address: HillK@techno.co.uk

Career objective

I am keen to launch a career in electrical engineering within the power industry. The organisation I am seeking is progressive and able to provide a comprehensive and structured learning programme, such as offered by ASM Power.

Skills, experience and personal attributes

Speaking and presentation skills

I am a confident and articulate public speaker. I was a finalist at the National University debating challenge held in Durham last year. In addition to this, I have presented to challenging academic panels on my university honours thesis. While at Dockley Power Station, I was required to present my findings from the testing and evaluation on a new type of pump under consideration by management. Following my evaluation and subsequent presentation, management at the Power Station went ahead with the purchase.

High computer literacy

I am a keen computer user and regularly use the following packages:

- CAD
- MS Excel 5.0
- MS Word 6.0a
- WordPerfect 6.1
- Netscape Navigator 3.0
- Eudora Light 3.0
- MS Project 4.0
- MS Powerpoint 4.0a

Willingness to embrace new ideas

My thesis topic, 'Power: It's a passion', looked at applications of current technology to the generation of power in the future. The industry journal *Engineers R US* contacted me to write an article around the topic with the editorial suggesting that some of the ideas were 'at the forefront of thinking around the topic'. Besides undertaking university studies, to keep my knowledge up-to-date I regularly undertake my own research via the Internet and numerous trade journals to determine industry trends and identify applications to my own work environment.

Education

Tertiary

1995 – 1998	Bachelor of Engineering (Electrical) Hons
	Salford University
	Honours Thesis: 'Power: It's a passion'

Secondary

1994	A levels: Maths, Economics, French, General Studies
	Pymble Ladies College

Academic achievements

1998	University Medal in Electrical Engineering
1998	Publication in *Engineering R US* entitled 'The Power or The Passion: Energy sources for the future'
1994	Rostrum Public Speaking Finalist
	Topic: 'Energy yesterday, today, tomorrow'.

Employment history

Nov 98 – Feb 99   Associate Electrical Engineer

Summer Vacation Student, Dockley Power Station, Armidale

Responsibilities

- assist electrical engineer in the design and lay-out of electrical installations and circuitry
- collect information, perform complex calculations and prepare diagrams and drawings of electrical installations and circuitry
- use CAD to produce designs and detailed drawings
- assist in testing and commissioning of electrical equipment and installations, and in the supervision of operations and maintenance.

Achievements

- new drawings for Dockley Power Station No. 1 completed
- pump re-designed and installation programme outlined

Interests and activities

University debating team, computer simulations, personal computing, cooking, hockey

Referees

Ms Lillian Salmon, Plant Manager, Dockley Power Station: (01924) 123456

Mr Tom Malone, Shift Supervisor, Dockley Power Station: (01924) 123457

Early career

FINANCIAL ACCOUNTANT

This is a fixed-term contract for a modern manufacturing site. Although supervising five people, the position is very much 'hands on' which requires a willingness to take on detail and the ability to juggle multiple tasks.

We seek a computer literate accountant, with experience of Microsoft systems and accounting experience which must include tax and general ledger. You will need to be a fully or part qualified accountant and possess strong written and verbal communication skills, ideally you will have manufacturing experience. However, it is unlikely that candidates with less than five years' accounting experience will have sufficient background for the position. This opportunity is available now.

Please call or send details to Mark Matthews,
Person Ltd, South St, Edinburgh EH4 3TL
Tel: (0131) 746 7132
Fax: (0131) 746 7123

Peter Plus

Address:	42 Lake View Drive	Telephone:	(0131) 236 1237
	Edinburgh EH1 2LP	Fax number:	(0131) 236 1238
		Mobile:	07127 83783
		Email address:	plus@vento.co.uk

Career objective

To secure a busy 'hands-on' senior financial role that provides challenge and capitalises on my accounting expertise.

Skills, experience and personal attributes

Accounting expertise

Having a varied finance background in both the public and private sector, I feel confident in my ability to fulfil the role of financial accountant as outlined. My experience in the taxation office has provided me with a thorough understanding of financial reporting requirements. While I have been at Helicopters Ltd, I have worked primarily in the areas of taxation and general ledger. My computing skills include use of Word for Windows, Excel and Access for reporting and record-keeping.

Attention to detail

Attention to detail is an essential performance criteria in my current role at Helicopters Ltd. I pride myself on delivering a quality reporting product that the management team can have confidence in. I cannot remember any instances where work has been returned to me for correction, or work has been withdrawn once errors were recognised. On my last staff appraisal, I was rated as 'Highly Commendable' on the criterion 'Attention to detail'.

Ability to manage multiple tasks

I have been required to work toward numerous and competing deadlines. Through careful planning and some delegation I have been successful in fulfilling all processing and reporting deadlines. Taking a team approach, where I manage the group's activity as well as actively participate in completing the work, I am able to get the best possible result.

Education

Tertiary

1983 – 1986   BA in Management Studies
                     University of Newcastle

Memberships

1988   Member, Institute of Chartered Accountants
1997   Member, Institute of Company Directors

Employment history

Dec 1993 – current Financial Controller, Helicopters Ltd, Haddington, Lothian

Responsibilities

- preparation, consolidation and review of management and project reporting
- overseeing the preparation of progress claims and analysis and reporting on cashflow
- controlling and covering all foreign exchange exposures
- ensuring that all insurance requirements for the project and contract are met
- liaison with banks for provision of security required under the contracts and subcontracts
- supervision of two accounting staff.

Achievements

- implemented new project reporting system to suit management team needs
- met all management reporting deadlines
- reduced time spent on compiling information in department by 65%
- substituted for company secretary in his absence.

Feb 89 – Nov 1993   Assistant Financial Controller, Helicopters Ltd

Responsibilities

- consolidation and preparation of management and statutory accounts, tax returns and budgets
- review and analysis of operating results for senior management
- overseeing the preparation of monthly board reports

- developing and implementing foreign exchange trading procedures and systems

- review and support of capital expenditure proposals.

Achievements

- implemented new foreign exchange trading procedures and systems

- all reporting deadlines met.

Dec 1986 – Jan 1989   Taxation Adviser, Tax Office, Edinburgh

Interests and activities

Gardening, sailing, golf, reading.

Referees

Ms Nancy Tam, Director of Finance, Helicopters Ltd: (0131) 672 4312

Mr Thomas Winter, Managing Director, Helicopters Ltd: (0131) 672 4313

Mid career

Training Manager
Handle Sisters Pharmaceuticals

Would you like to join the world's 3rd biggest pharmaceutical company, currently expanding rapidly in the European market? We require a manager to join our training division, where you would be responsible for the delivery of training programs to our sales staff.

A dynamic, results-focused team player, you will have excellent communications skills, and will be able to handle pressure and work to deadlines. With several years of solid experience in a multinational, you will be accredited in NLP and will have a basic understanding of training evaluation techniques. Reporting to our Regional Manager, you will be required to provide input into the marketing strategies for the European region by training our sales staff to improve market share.

Handle Sisters are Equal Opportunities employers.

Please forward your CV to: Linda Spark, Personnel Dept, Handle Sisters Pharmaceuticals, 58 Boundary Street, London EC1 2LP.

Josie Lee

Address: 15 Browns Rd
London NW2 4PT

Telephone: (020) 7124 5522
Fax number: (020) 7124 5523
Email: Josie@comten.com

Career objective

I am keen to build a career with a progressive learning organisation that genuinely values the contribution that training can make to achieving business objectives.

Skills, experience and personal attributes

Business acumen

In my current role at Fish Fingers Ltd. I am required to analyse business reports (e.g. sales, production) and identify training opportunities. By reviewing sales figures and talking to representatives I discovered that many were having trouble overcoming sales rejections. Training was designed to address this problem and sales increased by 25% two months after training. My practical experience is supplemented by graduate management qualifications from the University of London Business School.

Knowledge of training techniques

In addition to completing qualifications in adult education, I am an accredited NLP trainer (Level IV) and have conducted evaluations on all training courses conducted to date. As a member of the Institute of Training and Development, I undertake professional development so that I am continually updating my knowledge. In this way, I ensure that I maximise use of the best available training techniques.

Ability to motivate others

At FF Ltd training courses often need to be run after-hours or on weekends, cutting into sales representatives' personal lives. It is important from participants' perspectives that the courses are considered worthwhile, help them to deliver results on-the-job and are fun. To ensure that the trainees' needs were met, on appointment at FF Ltd I interviewed a cross-section of representatives, identified their needs and designed training courses to address these. Evaluations have proved these to be very successful with participant and manager satisfaction ratings of four and above for 85% of courses.

Education

Tertiary

1990 – 1993	BA (English)
	University of Wales, Cardiff
1994 – 1996	Graduate Management Qualification
	University of London Business School

Short courses

1997	NLP (Level IV) accreditation
	Training for Success
1998	New techniques in course evaluation
	Institute of Training and Development
1999	Games Trainers Play
	Training Mind-Gym Ltd

Academic achievements

1993	Best Trainer (as evaluated by practicum trainees)
	Awarded by the ITD

Employment history

Feb 1996 – current Training Manager, Fish Fingers Ltd, Brentford, Essex

Responsibilities

- identify training needs based on business objectives
- prepare business training plan
- design NLP-based training courses
- conduct training courses
- evaluate and report on learning outcomes
- manage training budget and expenditure
- manage department of three staff.

Achievements

- 80% of courses conducted out of core business hours to minimise selling downtime
- in-house designed sales training course contributed to 25% increase in sales
- participant and manager satisfaction ratings of four and above for 85% of courses
- training budget on target (£150,000) and expenditure on external consultants reduced by 18%.

Jan 1994 – Jan 1996   Training Officer, Baker's Dozen, West Ryde

Responsibilities

- evaluate off-the-shelf training courses and other training resources (e.g. videos)
- conduct off-the-shelf training courses
- prepare training materials
- report on training activity
- gather information on training needs
- evaluate in-house courses
- maintain training records.

Achievements

- implemented structured induction training courses for all new starters
- conducted courses according to training manager's training plan (on time and on budget).
- implemented new computerised training recordkeeping system.

Jan 1990 – Dec 1993   Crew Member, McDonald's, Cardiff

Interests and activities

Feb 1996 – current   FF Ltd Volleyball Team

Feb 1994 – Nov 1995   Baker's Dozen Volleyball Team

Feb 1990 – Nov 1993   Cardiff University Volleyball Team

Referees

Mr Milos Stefanovic, Director of Human Resources, Fish Fingers Ltd: (01694) 234 785

Ms Brigitte English, Training Manager, Baker's Dozen: (01415) 237 7412

Late career

GENERAL MANAGER – TECHNOLOGY

Our client, a leading national retailer, is seeking a General Manager to lead their business in a period of strong growth here in the UK and overseas.

The role

Principally the role will focus on developing a strategic IT plan that supports business objectives and future system requirements. There is a need to review and evaluate existing hardware/software and to manage a small support team.

The person

You are a business manager first and foremost who understands the retail industry. You have a thorough understanding of information technology, including current and future directions across the Internet/Intranet and Extranet. You possess strong people management skills and appreciate the importance of getting the best out of your staff. You have exceptional presentation skills and can tailor content to suit a broad audience. Excellent written presentation skills are required to communicate organisational needs and persuade senior management to implement system changes. This is an excellent opportunity for a successful individual to join a rapidly developing organisation and to make an impact on its future direction.

Send CV to:
Claudia Joy
Claudia Joy Ltd
PO Box 7
London WC1E 2PL

David Bussen

Address:	PO Box 321	Telephone:	(020) 7111 2345
	London WC1E 2AN	Fax number:	(020) 7111 2346
		Mobile:	07803 765123
		Email:	Bussen@hotmail.com

Career objective

To contribute to the successful growth and management of a retailing organisation by leading initiatives to link business needs with technological solutions.

Skills, experience and personal attributes

Leadership

As the group leader in Information Technology, I am required to identify the strategic technological and systems requirements of all retail stores. This is achieved by linking current and anticipated business needs with available technology. The Internet shopping site is a prime example of this. Leading a team of store managers, merchandising managers and IT managers we identified business needs, concerns and strategies. Under my leadership, the site was developed and launched within 18 months of conception.

Knowledge of the retail industry

I have worked in the retail industry for all of my working life, starting out at the bottom as a retail assistant, moving into a role as Customer Service Manager, leading an in-store IT team as the IT Manager and finally working my way up to a state-based corporate role. My unique grounding enables me to fully understand the day-to-day operations of a store as well as its management.

Business management

In my role as Senior Manager, New Technology, I am required to demonstrate a sound knowledge of each store's business requirements and strategic direction. I have supplemented my work experience with formal studies in a Masters of Business Administration. Key projects that I have been involved with that have resulted in both cost savings and efficiency improvements include fully integrated communications system and IT supplier resulting in an average cost saving of £500,000 per store; introduction of new technology to better monitor in-store trading patterns and provide links back to staffing requirements; implement new POS technology without disruption to trading pattern.

Education

Tertiary

1996 – 1998   Masters of Business Administration

Surrey University Business School

1989 – 1991   BSc – Information Technology

Newcastle University

1987 – 1988   Certificate IV – retail strategic management

Employment history

Dec 1994 – current   Senior Manager, New Technology, Faith Sisters Stores, Head Office

Duties include

- indirect responsibility for all in-store IT managers development of corporate IT plan
- management of corporate IT objectives
- monitoring of IT standards across stores
- identification and selection of hardware and software for stores in-house use
- implementation of new online shopping systems
- implementation of Intranet and video technology linking stores
- integration and selection of other new technology including POS, telephones, paging
- management team on-floor communication.

Achievements

- fully integrated communications system and supplier introduced to all stores over an 18-month period with an average cost saving of £500,000 per store
- all IT objectives outlined in 1998/9 corporate plan achieved

- introduction of weekly video conferencing with IT in-store managers to ensure sharing of best practice and improve communication
- on-line shopping system introduced returning £10 million in first week of operation with average growth of 15% per week and no loss of sales to individual stores.

Dec 1991 – Nov 1994   IT Manager, Faith Sisters Stores, Southern Region

Duties included

- management of IT team (3 staff)
- maintenance of in-store systems
- evaluation of software for store
- testing of new software for store
- implementation of new software
- implementation of back-up and recovery systems.

Achievements

- identified and introduced new technology 'Sales to Staffing' to better monitor in-store trading patterns and provide links back to staffing requirements
- implementation of new POS technology without disruption to trading pattern
- recovery systems worked in 100% of all cases, resulting in no down time due to computer failure
- recruited and developed own replacement over a two-year period.

Dec 1986 – Jan 1989   Customer Service Manager, Faith Sisters Stores, Southampton

Management of retail service team including

- staff scheduling
- performance management
- training and development
- monitoring service standards

- stock management and merchandising

- management of budgets for 'Homewares'

- management and staff utilisation reporting

- organising special product promotions.

Achievements

- budgets on target 85% of the time

- sales targets achieved and exceeded 85%

- named 'Customer Service Manager' of the year by the store manager

- successful selection and promotion of two staff members to the customer service manager traineeship.

Summary of other jobs

Dec 1984 – Nov 1986 Faith Sisters, Retail Assistant, Newcastle-upon-Tyne

Interests and activities

Squash, golf, Internet research of new products

Referees

Mr Tony Wilson, Director of IT, Faith Sisters Stores: (020) 7123 5432

Mr Graeme Kneebone, Managing Director, Faith Sisters Stores: (020) 7123 5435

**Returning after
a break**

COMPUTER ANALYST/PROGRAMMER

An outstanding opportunity exists to join our leading-edge Software Consultancy as an Analyst Programmer using the latest client/server technology. We are looking for creative and innovative thinkers who have a strong desire to be the best they can be in an environment that offers vast opportunities and rewards to dedicated and determined staff. You will be working and/or be trained alongside some of the best software developers in the field. Experience in Visual Basic, Access, SQL Server, and Internet development with tertiary qualifications would be highly regarded. If you are ambitious and have an enthusiastic personality, you are ideal for these challenging and exciting roles.

Top salary and remuneration, bonuses and incentives, with UK and/or international travel opportunities on offer to the right applicant/s.

Send CV to:
Human Resources Director
Softly Softly Ltd
Lock Hill St
Sheffield, S. Yorks
SH21 9PT

Jenny Barber

Address:	15 Fox Trot Boulevard	Telephone:	(020) 8123 7896
	Hackney, London E14 7AB	Fax number:	(020) 8123 7895
		Email:	jenny@messages.com

Career objective

To achieve my ultimate potential in an innovative and commercial environment that fully utilises my IT qualifications, experience and creativity.

Skills, experience and personal attributes

Ability to develop new products

I have previously written award winning and innovative software packages ('Ms Terry Investigates' and 'Y? Y? Y?') with sales of the latter package exceeding budget expectations by 150% (£2.3 million). During my university course, I have written two additional products judged by Human Side Ltd to be the best software products available of their kind. My course has provided me with up-to-date knowledge in Visual Basic, Access, SQL Server, and Internet technology.

Ambitious

With several years experience in programming and product development I am now keen to fulfil my ultimate potential in a demanding and challenging role at Softly, Softly Ltd. While at Educational Software Ltd, I was promoted from the role of programmer to senior programmer within two years based on my performance. When relocated with my partner to Albury, I took the opportunity to pursue relevant studies, so that up-to-date knowledge would help me to achieve my future career goals.

Knowledge of client/server technology

I led a project team exploring the application of client/server technology to a large telecommunications company. Using C/ST we were able to help the client to introduce a complex customer billing system that was simple and more cost effective. I am familiar with many of the client/servers and their capabilities through my own Internet research.

Education

Tertiary

1998 – 2000	BSc – Information Technology
	Napier University, Edinburgh
1985 – 1987	A-levels, North Leeds High School
	Subjects: Mathematics, IT, Geography, Business Studies

Academic achievements

1999	Best university software product
	Awarded by Human Side Ltd
1998	Best university educational software product
	Awarded by Human Side Ltd

Employment history

Feb 1994 – Dec 1997   Senior Programmer, Educational Software, Chatswood

Responsibilities

- as for 'Programmer' (see below) with additional responsibility for the supervision, development and performance management of 8 software programmers

Achievements

- team responsible for 7 award-winning packages during the period I was supervising
- sales of educational packages increased by 80% during the period I was supervising.

Feb 1992 – Jan 1994   Programmer, Educational Software, Chatswood

Responsibilities

- document computer users' requirements with analysts

- analyse objectives and software requirements identified by analysts

- write programs for educational software

- prepare support documentation for computer users and support personnel

- test and evaluate programs prepared by other programmers

Achievements

- wrote 'Ms Terry Investigates', winner of the 1997 educational software package of the year

- sales of educational package 'Y? Y? Y?' exceeded budget expectations by 150% (£2.3 million).

Jan 1991 – Jan 1992   PC Support Officer, Legal Eagles Ltd, London

Responsibilities

- software and hardware selection

- testing software prior to installation

- systems planning

- installation of software and hardware systems

- maintenance of systems

- basic programming

Achievements

- installation of major software upgrade (150 users) without loss of business trading time

- selection of software package that saved £50,000 in operating expenses.

Interests and activities

New Internet products, interactive computer games.

Referees

Ms Maggie Doyle, Sales Manager, Educational Software: (01456) 723045

Ms Nancy Downer, Director of IT, Educational Software: (01456) 723047

Career change

SALES REPRESENTATIVES

Deci Co. in Glasgow requires Sales Representatives to expand their sales to corporate clients. While experience in the printing industry is not essential, a proven sales and service ability in the above market would be a clear advantage. You should be highly motivated and focused on building a client base. You understand that success comes from building relationships with customers and tenaciously developing and promoting printing solutions to a wide industry client base. This position suits a practical results-driven achiever who seeks an attractive remuneration package.

Send CV to:
Douglas Giles, Giles Recruitment
PO Box 73
Glasgow
G73 2PU

Tim Dunham

Address:	West Wood Rd, Glasgow G3 3PA	Telephone:	(0141) 673 6291
		Fax number:	(0141) 673 6292
		Mobile:	(07709) 231527
		Email:	TimD@comten.co.uk

Career objective

I am keen to utilise my selling and customer service skills in a representative role that focuses on building relationships with existing customers, as well as translating opportunities into new accounts.

Skills, experience and personal attributes

Selling skills

In previous roles, I have been responsible for identifying new opportunities and developing strategies to turn these into reality. In my purchasing roles, I have been given a unique insight into your customer needs from their perspective. I understand the importance of their needs being identified, turning your product features into customer benefits and closing a deal that benefits both supplier and customer.

Customer service

By developing better relationships with vendors and suppliers I have been successful in generating significant improvements to customer service at Night Eye Cameras Ltd. I introduced a system to support the introduction of new products including better documentation, customer training and a customer hotline to deal with any product queries quickly. I believe that the key to good customer service is servicing existing clients as if you were trying to win their business for the first time. It is important to understand what is most important to them and then to address this need.

Highly motivated

I have achieved significant cost savings and efficiency improvements in previous positions and look forward to the opportunity to do the same thing for Deci Co. I establish goals for myself professionally and personally and then set about achieving these as quickly as possible. Promotions in previous positions have been the result of these efforts being recognised and rewarded.

Education

Tertiary

1997 – 1998   Associate Diploma of Business (Marketing)
                   Panorama College, Pollok

Short courses

1990   Purchasing Contract Negotiation
                   Institute of Purchasing Professionals
1993   Purchasing and Inventory Control Systems and Supply Management
                   Institute of Purchasing Professionals

Employment history

Jul 1992 – May 1997   Purchasing Manager, Night Eye Cameras Ltd

Responsibilities

- identify new opportunities and develop strategies to achieve business objectives
- develop and improve vendor relations
- implement procurement systems to maximise profit
- vendor management of contracts in excess of £12 million.

Achievements

- annual six digit savings in material expenditure
- successful negotiation of supply contracts with over 10 overseas vendors
- implement cost reduction techniques making Scottish-based manufacturing more cost effective than overseas contract assemblers
- implement a successful vendor assistance programme targeting new product support
- optimise storage facilities with the adoption of improved stock handling methods.

Oct 1989 – Jul 1992   Distribution Officer, Night Eye Cameras Ltd

Responsibilities

- rationalise distribution strategy
- develop methods to reduce product transit damage
- manage the inventory of product for under warranty/repair
- control international and national freight accounts
- coordinate dispatches to customers and sales offices worldwide.

Achievements

- consolidate freight services, resulting in an increase of bargaining power
- reduce transit damage to under 0.5%.

Jun 1988 – May 1989   Records Management, Sony Music

Apr 1985 – April 1988   Logistics/Supply Officer, Royal Navy

Interests and activities

- Rugby league, fishing, golf, personal computing

Referees

Mr Joshua Hill, Operations Director, Night Eye Cameras: (0131) 938 6142

Ms Jasmine Leggett, Sales Director, Night Eye Cameras: (0131) 938 6143

Now it's your turn

Using the foregoing examples as templates, you are now ready to complete your own CV. Go to it!

Blank templates to photocopy (enlarge to suit)

Template 1: Training template

Secondary/ Tertiary		Dates attended	From	To
Subjects studied	Results	Teams or clubs	Achievements	

Template 2: Jobs template

Employer 1

Employer Name and Address		Dates attended	From	To
Reason for leaving employer				

Job title	Dates	Key duties	Achievements/promotions

Training undertaken Title	Instructor/ organisation	Date	Description What I learned

Employer 2

Employer Name and Address		Dates attended	From	To
Reason for leaving employer				

Job title	Dates	Key duties	Achievements/promotions

Training undertaken Title	Instructor/ organisation	Date	Description What I learned

Template 3: Life template

Activity	Date	Description	Achievements/ personal development	Relevance to job applied for
Community work				
Hobbies/ Interests				
Sports				
Other				

CV howlers!

We asked a bunch of recruitment consultants to give us some examples of really terrible CVs. Here is what they said.

The ransom note

One was like a ransom note – letters and words cut out of the newspaper and stuck onto a sheet of paper.

The self-important scientist going for a non-science job

A scientist sent in a massive document about two centimetres thick with all their publications in it.

The runner-up

One had a load of sports certificates including their school high jump certificate – they hadn't even won. It was for second place!

Bodily fluids?

One with dog-eared corners that looked as though the dog had chewed it or the baby had vomited on it.

One with stains – where are the stains from?

The work of art

The desktop-published ones for advertising roles. Graphic designers are wonderful – they produce works of art that are like a sample of their work.

Personal photos taken in a photo booth. Ghastly.

The stripper

One listener phoned into a talkback interview we were giving and told the authors about the man who had his CV hand-delivered by a strip-a-gram.

Chequepoint Charlie

A bank manager made his CV out to look like a bank cheque, with the address appearing like the bank's address, and the telephone numbers as the cheque numbers.

The highrise CV

An architect produced a 3-D CV that was the perfect model of a house. On lifting the roof, each room contained different information on the candidate.

One size fits all

An applicant applied for every general manager's position advertised at the same company, regardless of the functional area, and sent the same poorly-typed standard (photocopied) letter of application plus a CV with a 'handwritten' reference to the position he was seeking.

For employers who have trouble reading the fine print

An applicant sent his entire CV in 16 point font so that it read like a kid's book.

A little too much information

This applicant felt the need to share all his secrets, including details of his haemorrhoids.

Where am I?

The applicant got the job title wrong (and we mean completely wrong) and then tailored the application to this wrong job.

Contact the author

Contact Jim Bright at jim@jimbright.com or www.jimbright.com.